Popular Music and Cultural Policy

Popular music is increasingly visible in government strategies and policies. While much has been written about the expanding flow of music products and music creativity in emphasising the global nature of popular music, little attention has been paid to the flow of ideas about policy formation and debates between regions and nations. This book examines specific regional and national histories, and the different cultural values placed on popular music. The state emerges as a key site of tension between high and low culture, music as art versus music as commerce, public versus private interests, the right to make noisy art versus the right to a good night's sleep. The political economy of urban popular music is a strong focus, examining attempts to combine and complement arts and cultural policies with 'creative city' and 'creative industries' strategies. The Anglophone case studies of policy contexts in Canada, Britain, the US and Australia reveal how the everyday influence and use of popular music is also about questions of aesthetics, funding and power.

This book was originally published as a special issue of the *International Journal of Cultural Policy*.

Shane Homan is an Associate Professor of Media Studies at Monash University, Melbourne, Australia.

Martin Cloonan is Professor of Popular Music and Politics at the University of Glasgow, Scotland, UK.

Jen Cattermole is a Lecturer in the Department of Music at Otago University, Dunedin, New Zealand.

Popular Music and Cultural Policy

Edited by
Shane Homan, Martin Cloonan and Jen Cattermole

LONDON AND NEW YORK

First published 2015
by Routledge
2 Park Square, Milton Park, Abingdon, Oxon, OX14 4RN, UK

and by Routledge
711 Third Avenue, New York, NY 10017, USA

Routledge is an imprint of the Taylor & Francis Group, an informa business

© 2015 Taylor & Francis

All rights reserved. No part of this book may be reprinted or reproduced
or utilised in any form or by any electronic, mechanical, or other means,
now known or hereafter invented, including photocopying and recording,
or in any information storage or retrieval system, without permission in
writing from the publishers.

Trademark notice: Product or corporate names may be trademarks or
registered trademarks, and are used only for identification and
explanation without intent to infringe.

British Library Cataloguing in Publication Data
A catalogue record for this book is available from the British Library

ISBN 13: 978-1-138-78776-6

Typeset in Times New Roman
by RefineCatch Limited, Bungay, Suffolk

Publisher's Note
The publisher accepts responsibility for any inconsistencies that may have
arisen during the conversion of this book from journal articles to book chapters,
namely the possible inclusion of journal terminology.

Disclaimer
Every effort has been made to contact copyright holders for their permission to
reprint material in this book. The publishers would be grateful to hear from any
copyright holder who is not here acknowledged and will undertake to rectify
any errors or omissions in future editions of this book.

Contents

Citation Information	vii
Notes on Contributors	ix

1. Introduction: popular music and policy   1
   Shane Homan, Martin Cloonan and Jen Cattermole

2. Music, markets and manifestos   7
   John Street

3. Irrational amusements, theatre law, and moral reformers in nineteenth-century
   America: implications for later popular music study   24
   Gillian Margaret Rodger

4. Steering a review: some reflections on a gig   44
   Martin Cloonan

5. Independent creative subcultures and why they matter   59
   Kate Shaw

6. 'Lend me your ears': social policy and the hearing body   79
   Bruce Johnson

7. Why get involved? Finding reasons for municipal interventions in the
   Canadian music industry   92
   Richard Sutherland

8. From Coombs to Crean: popular music and cultural policy in Australia   108
   Shane Homan

Index   125

Citation Information

The chapters in this book were originally published in the *International Journal of Cultural Policy*, volume 19, issue 3 (June 2013). When citing this material, please use the original page numbering for each article, as follows:

Chapter 1
Introduction: popular music and policy
Shane Homan, Martin Cloonan and Jen Cattermole
International Journal of Cultural Policy, volume 19, issue 3 (June 2013) pp. 275–280

Chapter 2
Music, markets and manifestos
John Street
International Journal of Cultural Policy, volume 19, issue 3 (June 2013) pp. 281–297

Chapter 3
Irrational amusements, theatre law, and moral reformers in nineteenth-century America: implications for later popular music study
Gillian Margaret Rodger
International Journal of Cultural Policy, volume 19, issue 3 (June 2013) pp. 298–317

Chapter 4
Steering a review: some reflections on a gig
Martin Cloonan
International Journal of Cultural Policy, volume 19, issue 3 (June 2013) pp. 318–332

Chapter 5
Independent creative subcultures and why they matter
Kate Shaw
International Journal of Cultural Policy, volume 19, issue 3 (June 2013) pp. 333–352

Chapter 6
'Lend me your ears': social policy and the hearing body
Bruce Johnson
International Journal of Cultural Policy, volume 19, issue 3 (June 2013) pp. 353–365

CITATION INFORMATION

Chapter 7

Why get involved? Finding reasons for municipal interventions in the Canadian music industry
Richard Sutherland
International Journal of Cultural Policy, volume 19, issue 3 (June 2013) pp. 366–381

Chapter 8

From Coombs to Crean: popular music and cultural policy in Australia
Shane Homan
International Journal of Cultural Policy, volume 19, issue 3 (June 2013) pp. 382–398

Please direct any queries you may have about the citations to
clsuk.permissions@cengage.com

Notes on Contributors

Jen Cattermole is a Lecturer in the Department of Music at Otago University, Dunedin, New Zealand. Her primary field of research is ethnomusicology, with a particular focus on Maori and Pacific Islander music.

Martin Cloonan is Professor of Popular Music and Politics at the University of Glasgow, UK. His main research interest lies in the politics of popular music, involving issues such as censorship and freedom of expression.

Shane Homan is an Associate Professor of Media Studies at Monash University, Melbourne, Australia. He has written extensively about the contemporary music industries.

Bruce Johnson is a Professor in the Department of Media, Music, Communication and Cultural Studies at Macquarie University, Sydney, Australia. His main research interests are sound as cultural history, Australian popular music, particularly jazz, and musical diasporas.

Gillian Margaret Rodger is an Associate Professor of musicology and ethnomusicology at the University of Wisconsin-Milwaukee, USA. Her research focuses on the popular musical theatre of nineteenth-century America.

Kate Shaw is based at the School of Land and Environment at the University of Melbourne, Australia. She has a particular interest in Melbourne's live music and indie arts scenes, and advises governments and local campaigns on planning and policies to maintain them.

John Street is Professor of Politics at the University of East Anglia, Norwich, UK. His research focuses on the politics of media and culture.

Richard Sutherland is Assistant Professor in the Department of Policy Studies at Mount Royal University, Calgary, Canada. In particular, his work has focused on the music industry in Canada and its interactions with government policy from the 1960s onward.

Introduction: popular music and policy

Shane Homan[a], Martin Cloonan[b] and Jen Cattermole[c]

[a]Faculty of Arts, Research Unit in Media Studies, Monash University, Caulfield, Australia; [b]School of Culture and Creative Arts, University of Glasgow, Research Unit in Media Studies, Glasgow, Scotland; [c]Department of Music, University of Otago, Dunedin, New Zealand

> This special issue derives from the conference *Policy Notes: Popular Music, Industry and the State* hosted by the issue editors in Melbourne, 18–20 June 2012. The conference marked the completion of a three-year Australian Research Council project, *Policy Notes: Local Popular Music in Global Creative Economies* that examined popular music policy in Scotland, New Zealand and Australia. The issue offers several case studies examining how local music-making has become part of creative industries practices and policies, and the challenges faced by the music industries and governments in the funding, regulation and management of popular music.

Introduction: popular music and cultural policy

This special issue derives from the conference *Policy Notes: Popular Music, Industry and the State* hosted by the issue editors in Melbourne, 18–20 June 2012. The conference marked the completion of a three-year Australian Research Council project *Policy Notes: Local Popular Music in Global Creative Economies* that examined music policy in Scotland, New Zealand and Australia. As project researchers and conference organisers, we wished to not only share some of our project themes and concerns with like-minded practitioners, but also expand and reinforce contacts between disparate popular music policy researchers located across various disciplines and regions. To our knowledge, this gathering was the first conference of its kind in explicitly focusing on music policy, and we were especially mindful of the need to invite music industry and government figures where applicable to ensure that different research and policy communities spoke to each other.

The conference hosted presentations from Australia, New Zealand, Canada, Scotland, England and the US, with a significant presence from Australian government and industry policy-makers in the audience and behind the lectern. It proved to be useful in the presentation of an array of academic approaches, including cultural studies, human geography, popular music studies, musicology and media studies. Unfortunately, several presenters from other regions (South Africa, Asia) withdrew from the conference due to travel funding problems, a reminder that (white) academics in Western universities remain in privileged positions to collaborate through the support of institutions that remain relatively well funded and supportive of such exercises. Yet the distinct Anglophone bias at the conference also reflected the origins of popular music policy research. Britain has enjoyed a strong interest in music policy that surfaced (sometimes indirectly) through sociology and cultural studies research. In similar ways, it is understandable that Britain's 'colonies', with national government structures replicating the UK, have also produced strong cultural/music policy research, where the state remains a dominant player. This is especially evident in Australia, where the export of UK policy research themes extended to academics such as Colin Mercer and Tony Bennett moving to Australian universities, contributing to significant cultural policy work since the mid-1990s (see *Media Information Australia*'s 'Policy Moment' issue of 1994). Further efforts must be made to engage with emerging music policy researchers in other regions, especially where 'creative industry' strategies are being developed for the first time.

A central aim of the conference was to consider both the macro and micro activities and contexts of policy. While much has been written about the expanding flow of music products and music creativity in emphasising the global nature of popular music, little attention has been paid to the flow of ideas about policy formation and debates between regions and nations. The conference also produced meaningful engagement between researchers about city policies, especially as more local governments aspire to brand themselves as 'music capitals' of their state or region. This was linked to the ubiquitous presence of 'creative city' strategies in different nations.

As with the conference, this special issue considers popular music policy as a separate sphere of study that nonetheless retains intimate links with cultural policy studies. As Hesmondhalgh (2013, p. 167) points out, the definition of cultural policy in Anglophone contexts often simply refers 'to the subsidy, regulation and management of the arts'. Several of the articles presented here show that subsidy questions remain, although in different ways to earlier periods, as popular music raises its voice to compete with the high arts for funding (and popular music subsidy is increasingly likely to appear across other non-arts departments, such as youth or health).

Former controversies about the place of popular music at the policy table have now receded, replaced by more detailed debates and increasingly complex funding arrangements that attempt to combine and complement arts and cultural policies with industry/business strategies. Yet other articles reveal that much of the policy tension remains in regulation, where governments continue to display schizophrenic attitudes, encouraging popular music through subsidy (of venues, touring, recording) and restricting popular music at the same time through regulation (zoning, licensing, noise or media laws). The collection of articles here also reflects the shift in the 1990s to the larger role of popular music in cultural city planning. For many local governments, especially those administering the larger regional and national capitals, it is not a question of whether to encourage popular music, but how and by how much. At the local level, creative industries policy is increasingly meshing with urban policies to produce branding strategies in the race to be proclaimed a 'music capital', as Austin, Texas, has done through a series of explicit popular music policies, capped by investment in a globally acknowledged music industry festival, south by south-west.

This is not to say that the value placed on popular music is not contentious. In 'music, markets and manifestos', John Street considers popular music policy in one sense as simply indicative of all policy-making, in resolving the same questions, including the allocation of limited funds and resources, and the competing demands on importance and priority. Street (and all the authors in this issue) reinforces the highly political nature of cultural policy, despite politicians' repeated claims to govern from distinct value positions. How value is placed upon music is a central theme of Street's article, as a barometer of how popular music is now represented as an economic or social good. The article examines that confronting all cultural activity: how is culture – in this case, popular music – to be valued (and a rather different set of questions to how it should be measured). Street presents a series of case studies that expose different economic, political and aesthetic arguments. Despite politicians' occasional attempts to produce landmark statements about their culture or arts portfolios, definitive value judgements about the role and place of music in contemporary life, detached from their market or economic value, are rare. Instead, Street believes this absence is best filled through the production of values based around music's relationship to human and cultural rights, especially as a counterweight to instrumentalist discourses.

Gillian Rodger's article is an account of nineteenth-century values relating to popular culture that reminds us that live entertainment has a long and controversial history. Rodgers presents a series of US city case studies from the 1800s in which theatre and music hall entertainment confronted the moral certainties of city administrators. In these cases, concerns were firmly drawn upon class lines, with the 'lower' music hall and saloon entertainments viewed dimly against those theatres offering plays and musicals of the day. Rodgers' case studies reveal several themes: consistent government desires to encourage the *correct* mix of patrons and populations (discouraging the mingling of men and women, and especially prostitution); the corralling where possible of 'low entertainments' in hidden/poorer parts of the city; and keeping an ever watchful eye on the role of alcohol in venue profits and popularity. The subsequent role of licensing to subdue the stage where other ordnances had failed is a strategy familiar to musicians and policy workers within contemporary live music industries. Apart from clearly showing an earlier period of moral panic where 'respectable' became the defining discourse for active legislative prohibition against the 'popular', Rodgers' piece also has contemporary resonance for city planners who vainly hope that entertainment can always be contained so that 'art' can flourish.

While the number of academics involved in industry and policy work in popular music is increasing, reflection about the proper role of the academic in industry-policy circuits is surprisingly scarce. In 'Steering a Review', Martin Cloonan offers an interesting account of his participation in a Steering Group as part of a commissioned review of the music sector in Scotland. It is a forceful reminder of the many constituencies that such a gathering of 'experts' must serve: the many different sectors of a national popular music industry, often with competing agendas, and a range of government sectors, who also have competing visions. The 'background noise' is often as important as the 'foreground' responsibilities. Cloonan reveals the distinctive background noise in this case: a cultural industry that remains largely governed from Westminster, but contemplating financial and legislative independence; and the recent creation of Creative Scotland that incorporated previously independent bodies and industry groups. The article is a useful example of how the fundamental principles of research are viewed differently by the academy, government and industry, and Cloonan raises important questions about notions of independence and the difficulties of engaging in activist policy work that is not afraid to remain disinterested from particular industry and government agendas. These debates have occurred within cultural policy studies (see e.g. Bennett 2007, Schlesinger 2009); it is time they were revisited in the context of popular music policy.

One of the central engines of popular music pleasure, and industry growth, has been 'indie' (independent) music subcultures (see e.g. Kruse 1993). Distinctive music scenes (Straw 1991) provide impetus along a range of activities: the importance of a venue that caters to local acts and allows emerging musicians to experiment and find an audience; the local radio station which airs local acts as a buffer against the determinedly commercial offerings of mainstream stations; or even a local rehearsal studio or café that becomes a hub for meeting and finding like-minded fans, musicians and knowledge. In this issue, Kate Shaw explores the contemporary importance of indie subcultures within Melbourne, Australia. In contrast to most case studies of this kind that focus upon the interactions of specific indie infrastructure, Shaw has taken a macro view, tracing the history and geography of indie subcultures within Melbourne of the 1990s and 2000s. Her argument is different from the current thinking of many city/cultural planners who often favour large, symbolic arts and cultural infrastructure as centrepiece demonstrations of how a city 'gets' music. As Shaw reveals, this has been at the continual expense of smaller, less glamorous indie activity. As with Cloonan's piece, the 'background noise' is also critical here: combinations of increasing rent, which in turn lead to changes in land use (especially gentrification), are the drivers behind a gradual but persistent shift in indie clusters of activity from south to north of the Melbourne CBD. Shaw's research has many implications for urban cultural planning and music's place in the 'creative city', not the least of which is how to achieve the right mix of places and spaces that calls for a holistic government approach to housing, licensing, retail and zoning policy as much as traditional cultural funding.

Bruce Johnson's article in this issue explores some interesting questions about the future place of popular music in the city. As Johnson points out, the patterns and types of music use across urban environments – personal systems such as the iPod, the larger PA systems of commercial dance parties, the increasing volume of music within and outside homes and apartments – are not often explored by popular music researchers more frequently concerned with the sociological/cultural effects of such activity. His article examines the increasing problems associated with Low Frequency Noise across various city and global contexts. Residential noise complaints about living room stereo or amplified pub music remains a problem for both industries and governments, with the lower end of the decibel spectrum (the bass guitar, bass drum) a primary offender in penetrating home or street soundscapes. Johnson reveals how this is exacerbated by current planning controls that privilege dense high-rise development of mixed use. The article is a call for popular music researchers to begin working more closely with environmental noise experts to further understanding of the technical and social effects of increasing decibel levels.

Richard Sutherland also adopts a city case study approach in his examination of local popular music policy in Calgary, Canada. As a country with more success than most in enacting a range of national funding and broadcasting policies for popular music, Sutherland outlines the ways in which local policies are thin on the ground, obstructed by federal law and traditions and limited means of generating income. Nonetheless, Calgary is keen to explore strategic measures, driven in part by municipal envy: the wider reputation and infrastructure of Toronto (also explored here) as a 'music city'. What Sutherland details is an interesting mixture of public policies that are at times at odds with each other, in similar ways to Rodgers' history of nineteenth-century US cities. In this case, public funds develop new venues, while zoning laws remove others; and a music city strategy of sorts is developed without any input from the local and national music industries. The article points to the often underestimated difficulties of city councils in encouraging popular music in ways that do not duplicate national instruments and the extent to which local policies are explicitly 'cultural' or 'industrial' in form.

The tensions between cultural and industrial policies is a focus of Shane Homan's article tracing the history of popular music and related policies in Australia from the 1970s, and the gradual means by which popular music was incorporated within arts policies. This required not the abandonment of initial policies and funding backing the opera, musical or symphony concert, but for spaces to be found where popular music could be justified as worthy of support. By the late 1980s, popular music was enjoying limited federal government support that connected with youth, export and employment strategies, supplemented by local content quota laws for radio and television broadcasting that ensured local musicians were seen and heard. However, as Homan argues, older and simpler policies in the name of cultural protection are giving way to more complex policy questions derived from media and cultural convergence. This includes the re-examination of high arts funding and governance predicated upon 'excellence' discourses (see Street, this issue; Loosely 2011). Homan's piece raises a series of questions about the future role and definition of the nation state in music policy formation (cf. Cloonan 2007), and where and how Australian governments, musicians and fans will continue to see evidence of 'the national' on their (television, mobile phone and tablet) screens and in the venues.

Conclusion

The articles gathered here show that popular music is now the focus of concerted policy initiatives across the globe. Sometimes these are active attempts to promote, at other times efforts to constrain. More often, popular music may be caught up in policy decisions focused elsewhere but with enormous implications for it. Education, copyright legislation and urban planning (which can affect venues) provide just three obvious examples of this. Within all this, the state emerges as a key site for the playing-out of various seeming dichotomies – high versus low culture, music as art versus music as commerce, public versus private interest, the right to make noisy art versus the right to a good night's sleep. Politicians enter debates with their own vested interests, and the state retains the capacity to oppress as well as support artistic endeavours. Given the myriad ways in which citizens come into contact with popular music every day, it is little surprise that it remains an area of contestation around aesthetics, funding and power. Academics also rarely enter this arena without their own policy objectives and desired outcomes. The task of the popular music policy researcher remains to illuminate and to argue. We hope that this edition provides ammunition for both.

References

Bennett, T., 2007. *Critical trajectories: culture, society, intellectuals*. Malden, MA: Blackwell.

Cloonan, M., 2007. *Popular music and the state in the UK: culture, trade or industry?* Aldershot: Ashgate.

Hesmondhalgh, D., 2013. *The cultural industries*. Los Angeles, CA: Sage.

Kruse, H., 1993. Subcultural identity in alternative music culture. *Popular music*, 12 (1), 33–41.

Loosely, D., 2011. Introduction. Special issue, popular culture. *International journal of cultural policy*, 17 (4), 361–364.

Media Information Australia, 1994. Policy moment issue. 73, August.

Schlesinger, P., 2009. Creativity and the experts: new labour, think tanks and the policy process. *International journal of press politics*, 14 (3), 16–32.

Straw, W., 1991. Systems of articulation, logics of change: communities and scenes in popular music. *Cultural studies*, 5 (3), 368–388.

Music, markets and manifestos

John Street

School of Political, Social and International Studies and ESRC Centre for Competition Policy, University of East Anglia, Norwich, UK

This article is about the value of music, measured not in aesthetic terms, but rather as a matter of practical politics. The question of cultural value is, of course, familiar to those who study cultural policy. Typically, the political debate divides between (1) those who argue that music must take its chance in the market, where its value will be revealed in the price consumers are willing to pay; (2) those who see music as having social value, beyond that realised in the market, but seek to measure that value in terms recognised by economists (e.g. Contingent Valuation); and finally (3), those who reject the economistic route, and argue that music's value is of a different order and kind. What can get overlooked in this debate, and why it can be so frustrating, is the politics that underlies it – the politics of power and policy-making, and the politics of principle. This article argues that we should focus more explicitly on the politics, seeing culture – in this case, music – as a political resource and the bearer of political values, and to see music policy as an articulation of political value as much as of cultural value.

Introduction

This article is about how the value of music is constituted politically. This is important, I want to suggest, to debates about the value of culture and the policies that enshrine this value. Cultural policy – like all forms of policy – is about allocating scarce resources and resolving competing demands, and is intensely political (in the sense that politics is about who gets what, when and how). Cultural policy is also about attributing value to the objects of cultural policy – the artistic and cultural forms that are supported and regulated (and the means by which they are supported and regulated). My suggestion is that culture-as-art is not simply a matter of aesthetics, but is constituted routinely as a political good to which political value attaches as part of the experiences and ideas it embodies. Seeing culture as politically constituted is key to the debate about the value of culture and to the practice of cultural policy-making.

My focus throughout is on music. Although there may be a case for treating music as in some way 'special', that is not my concern here. Music serves merely as a case study of a broader set of claims. These have to do with the ways in which political value is invested in music and becomes intrinsic to our understanding of it. I want to suggest that music is more than the object of policy; it is the embodiment of rights and freedoms. This is not to deny that music is also the object of policy and the object of market exchanges. Rather, it is to argue that what is traded or regulated is also the bearer of political value.

This is not, of course, a universally shared view. For example, Mill (1989/1869), one of the founding figures of modern liberalism, refers to music as a 'taste' that – like smoking – can be adopted or discarded at will. For him, it is of minimal importance in itself. But there are others for whom music carries political weight. Mill's indifference can be contrasted with the views of the contemporary political philosopher Nussbaum (2001), who places music at the centre of her account of human emotion and human flourishing, and the place of both in the moral and political order. Another political philosopher Sandel (2012) writes in his recent book, *What Money Can't Buy*, about the pricing and availability of tickets for a Bruce Springsteen concert. He does so in order to illustrate the importance of non-monetary values to the quality of human life and to democracy. For Sandel, the 'good' that is realised in a Springsteen concert cannot be accounted in purely cash terms. It lives in the communal experience and understandings that exist outside the reach of market value. I will return to this argument at the end. All I am doing here is suggesting that, while music may be a matter of indifference to some political philosophers, it can assume a significance that goes well beyond that assigned to mere preferences and tastes.

At the same time, I am wary of making music a magical entity that exists beyond the material world. Music is also a commercial product, exchanged in the market place, and hence is valued in monetary terms too. By way of a reminder, here is how a record industry executive explained the modern route to market:

> We have an artist portal which is part of a hypercubic database … It's a real-time system that analyses live information from business partners – so that's all the sales data from a la carte services, all the data coming in from the streaming services; it does real-time analysis of Vevo plays, real-time analysis of Facebook and twitter sentiment analysis. (Rob Wells, President of Global Digital Business, Universal, quoted in Forde 2012, p. 68)

What is being described here are the latest means for monitoring consumer taste and delivering goods that satisfies it. But while these apparently sophisticated practices are core parts of the music business, it does not mean that music can itself be reduced to commercial transactions. Or rather, the transactions are about more than the bottom line. This thought is neatly captured by the commentator Willis (2011, n.p.) writing in the 1970s:

> The distinctive aesthetic of mass art, which is based on images (and sounds) designed to have an intense sensory, erotic, and emotional impact, clearly derives from the necessities of marketing – the need to distinguish one product from its competitors, to grab and hold the largest possible audience. But the forms invented to fulfill those requirements – the bright colors, bold, linear patterns, and iconic simplicity of advertising art, the sexual rhythms, tight construction, irresistible hook lines, and insistent repetition of rock-and-roll songs – have an autonomous aesthetic existence. They convey their own message, which, like the content of advertising (or the content of pop lyrics), is essentially hedonistic.

Willis's point, and it is, of course, not unique to her, is that, in the very business of competing in the market place, musical products acquire (or seek to acquire) features that distinguish them from their rivals and which give them value that cannot be cashed out in purely commercial terms.

It is in this context that music policy operates, at the intersection of aesthetic value and commercial logic. Cultural and commercial values are negotiated in policy. This is the business of politics, where politics refers both to the routines of resource distribution and to the attribution of value.

Politics and the value of culture

Giving a value to culture is nothing new. But equally it is a practice to which there is no settled answer. By way of illustration, consider recent thinking within the UK's Department of Culture, Media and Sport (DCMS). In 2009, the DCMS, in conjunction with the Arts and Humanities Research Council and the Economic and Social Research Council (ESRC), appointed an academic researcher to a placement fellowship. The topic of the fellowship was 'Measuring the value of culture'. It was awarded to Dave O'Brien (2010, p. 12), who argued in his final report that culture has to be given an economic value. To not do so would be to effectively remove culture from the list of priorities for public spending. If it is not possible to give culture a value, how can it be weighed in the balance of competing claims on the public purse? This is not an argument for the market as the arbiter of all decisions. Rather it is a *political* argument that if the culture lobby refuses to engage in debates about the economic value of culture (including music), their claims will be ignored by those with the power to set public priorities. O'Brien is insistent that the culture lobby has to confront a political reality in which resources are scarce and where economics provides a basis for determining how those scarce resources be divided up.

In making this case, O'Brien has in mind those who want to resist the suggestion that culture can be valued in this way. O'Brien quotes several examples of this kind of argument. The first trades on the claim that art's value is not to be understood in instrumental terms. O'Brien (2010, p. 12) quotes John Tusa (one time BBC presenter and executive, and ex-Managing Director of the Barbican Arts Centre): 'Mozart is Mozart because of his music and not because he created a tourist industry in Salzburg or gave his name to decadent chocolate and marzipan Saltzburger kugel'. Tusa's argument is that art's value is 'intrinsic'; it defies any attempt to place an economic value (or any other measurable quantity). It is understood to 'enrich lives', but how it does this cannot be documented, or at least not in ways that can feed into a cost-benefit analysis in which means and ends can be measured. Furthermore, according to the argument for art's intrinsic value, art represents the problem of 'incommensurability'; there is no standard of comparison by which different works of art can be compared. O'Brien quotes the following example of this kind of argument: 'How many Gershwin songs sum up to a Shostakovich symphony? Is a Haydn string quartet better than a Hemmingway short story? How does a Blake poem compare to a modern ballet performance?' (ibid.) According to advocates of the view that art's value is 'intrinsic', such questions are unanswerable. There is no measure or metric that is able to capture the qualities understood to inhere in a piece of art or music.

O'Brien despairs of such arguments because they refuse to recognise the reality of politics and policy-making. Given a world of finite resources, any policy community must fight its corner against its rivals, and must compete under the terms set by the key arbiter, the purse holder – in the UK, the Treasury. The Treasury insists that all policy demands are to be assessed by cost benefit analysis (CBA), the principles of which are set out in the so-called Green Book (http://www.hm-treasury.gov.uk/data_greenbook_index.htm). The 2012 edition of the Green Book makes specific reference to the possibility of applying CBA to non-market goods such as the environment or culture. O'Brien's argument – and it has proved to be an influential one – is that arts organisations and their supporters must engage with CBA if they are to hope to secure state funding (and support more generally) for the arts. This means that any cultural initiative has to be assessed in terms of the benefits it provides and the costs it imposes.

It is, however, one thing to argue for the need to engage in arguments about the value of art, and not to try to avoid this by claims about the uniqueness, ineffability or incommensurability of the art, but it is quite another to concede that CBA provides the best method (both technically and politically) to determine the value of that art and to determine what policies are appropriate to it. What I want to suggest is that the business of allocating and setting priorities needs to be recognised as involving political trade-offs, rather than cost-benefit ones. The value of music (and culture more generally) needs to be debated in explicitly political terms. This does not mean that arguments about art should be seen as either squabbles between competing ideological positions, although that may be involved, nor between competing interests (and their associated power), although this may be entailed as well. My argument is that music is itself a source of political value, and the question is how we understand and assess that value which is what is entailed by the making of cultural policy. The rest of this paper is about what this might possibly mean and what its implications are for music policy. My aim, I should add, is not to provide an answer that speaks in general or abstract terms about the value of music. Instead, my concern is with the practical implications of attributing a value to music in a world of finite resources and competing political priorities.

Arguing about music policy: two examples

To give a sense of the argument behind this paper, and its practical context, let me give two examples of arguments about music policy. Both involve the BBC. The first concerns its decision to close its 6Music channel. The second has to do with its rationale for the DJ (Chris Moyles) who, until late 2012, presented its flagship Breakfast Show on Radio 1.

The case of 6Music

In early 2011, the BBC threatened to close its 6Music service. There was an outcry (one that spread well beyond its very modest audience). 6Music is one of the BBC's digital channels; it plays music not typically heard on the mainstream popular music channels, Radios 1 and 2. One of the spokespeople for the campaign against closure was the musician and 6Music DJ, Jarvis Cocker, who offered this defence:

> The show that I do couldn't exist on any other station. I'm allowed to play whatever music I like, interview whoever I like and record jingles in my cellar. The presenters

of 6Music are music makers as well as music presenters. The BBC must offer licence players value for money and I'm not saying what we get paid but they do it for the love of music and it is certainly value for money. 6Music is never going to be the biggest station in the UK but it would be devastating if it was to close. 6Music isn't going to change the world, it just wants to make it a bit nicer. (quoted in 'Jarvis Cocker rants against 6Music closure', Daily Telegraph, 11th May 2010)

Making the world a 'nicer' place may be a worthy aim, but it hardly constitutes the most powerful of arguments, and it is very unlikely that, when 6Music was indeed saved, that this was because of the station's 'niceness'. More likely, it was reprieved because of more robust arguments and their well-placed advocates. The evidence supplied by organisations such as the copyright collecting society PRS for Music emphasised the commercial value of 6Music to the UK music industry. This value lay in 6Music's capacity to generate income for more songwriters than did any other channel (Page 2010). There were good, economic or commercial reasons for maintaining 6Music.

Pay the DJ: what is Chris Moyles worth?

Not all arguments about music policy need, though, to be about money – even when this appears to be the focus of the discussion. This is illustrated by my second example. It concerns the salary paid to the BBC DJ Chris Moyles. Moyles, who has since moved on, hosted the breakfast show for Radio 1. His audience was large (c12 million weekly listeners).

The question of what Moyles was worth was raised by the tabloid press, who deemed him worth much less than his reported annual salary of £600,000. For several media commentators, there was no conceivable rationale for paying Moyles this much. The prevalent assumption was that being a DJ demanded little in the way of talent, and that licence fee money could be better spent. (There was, of course, a further agenda: the persisting demand that the BBC's popular music provision be 'privatised' to reduce the size of the BBC's overall budget and its overbearing presence in the media market).

How did the BBC respond? Not by discussing Moyles's salary, which remained confidential. Rather, the BBC advanced a number of different arguments (e.g. BBC 2008, BBC Trust 2011). Firstly, they drew attention to his 'popularity'. This was measured in terms of listeners, but also in terms of the other forms of interaction that Moyles had with his audience. Secondly, the BBC drew attention to his 'representativeness' – that he spoke from and for his audience. Thirdly, wary that ratings were not in themselves a validation of public service broadcasting (PSB), the BBC suggested that Moyles acted as a 'conduit', bringing his young audience into contact with Radio 1's PSB obligation to inform and educate, as well as entertain. He linked them to Newsbeat, the R1 news service, and to the various documentaries and other services (employment, education, health, etc.) that the corporation provided. And finally, the BBC drew attention to Moyles's contribution to British music: while he played fewer new tracks than his colleagues, he played more *British* ones. To this extent, Moyles helped the BBC to deliver on its PSB commitments to promote UK musical talent.

The BBC's arguments did not focus on the economic benefits that Moyles represented, although there was the suggestion that he contributed to the health of the UK music industry (much as it was claimed that 6Music did). What the Corporation did suggest, however, was that the value of Moyles, and the music that he played, was to be measured instrumentally, in the capacity to realise other goods and goals. Moyles's role (and hence his salary) was justified by his ability to deliver specific ends (audience reach, public service and assisting the UK music industry).

What is involved here extends beyond Chris Moyles's salary (or the survival of 6Music). It is about the rationale for public provision of commercially produced popular music. The issue that lies unaddressed in all the BBC's defence of Moyles is whether there is any compelling reason for popular music to be provided by a publicly funded broadcaster, and more broadly whether there is any necessity in the good society for music to be the object of public policy. Faced with these questions, are we driven to arguments of the kind that O'Brien derides – about the ineffable, incomparable and intrinsic value of music? Or can we establish a case for music's value that might: (a) be recognised by Treasury civil servants (and that it is not simply an instrument in some other policy agenda); and (b) meets the concerns of those who see music as having a value that cannot be captured by cost-benefit analysis – what Bostridge (2011) calls its 'magic'? My suggestion is that we can, but that in doing so we need to recognise its *political* constitution and value. It is only by this route that we can mount an argument (and an associated political legitimacy) that both accords music a value that justifies its public provision. This is to borrow an argument by Keat (2011), who contends that the public provision of a good or service requires for its defence either that it promotes justice and fairness, or that it provides a higher quality than would be available by other (market) means. In what follows, I examine the problems of making such a case for music by considering two different approaches – which are labelled for simplicity's sake the 'economic' and the 'political' arguments – to establishing the case for the public provision of music. The first of these is that preferred by O'Brien in his recommendations to the DCMS.

The economic argument

O'Brien opted for contingent valuation (CV) as his method for accommodating the demands of a policy process based on cost-benefit analysis. CV allows culture (or music) to feature in the policy evaluation methods adopted by the Treasury by generating a proxy value for non-market goods like culture or nature. These values are obtained through the use of surveys in which citizen-consumers are asked to report their willingness-to-pay for goods and services that are not susceptible to market exchange. The CV approach is a widely used method – to estimate the value of the natural realm such as the Alps, or of the cultural realm, such as public service broadcasting or the theatre. Over the forty years or so that CV methods have been used, some very stringent protocols have been introduced to ensure their robustness (see Noonan 2003, for one survey). Despite this, CV remains controversial. One of the criticisms is that it reduces policy-making to a purely technical exercise, one to be left to technocrats.

Frey (2003, p. 196), for example, argues that CV fails to acknowledge the political dimensions of cultural decisions: 'Willingness-to-pay procedures, and in particular CV, are useful but have a decisive disadvantage: they are not directly related to political decisions'. Although CV establishes a value for any given non-market goods, it does not translate into a rank ordering, or a system for determining how competing claims might be resolved. For this reason, Frey suggests that the political dimension be supplied by the use of referenda. He writes: 'Popular referenda combine the evaluation of competing alternatives with democratic decisions. This combination is particularly relevant and beneficial for cultural decisions' (ibid.). Democracy provides a means of weighing the alternative non-market goods.

Frey also holds that democracy provides a guarantee of artistic freedom. His claim here is that, while dictatorships may produce a greater variety of culture (and be less subject to a populist tendency towards the average), democracy is key to preserving artistic freedom. 'In our modern world', he writes:

> where the population as a whole, and in particular artists, have experienced a rise in self-determination brought about by democracy, a decision-making system involving the whole population is by far the best-equipped to establish, and to safeguard, constitutional rights for artistic freedom. (2003, p. 17)

But such methods, while they may be able to evaluate particular forms of culture, cannot provide any guidance as to the principles upon which culture should be regulated or administered. They cannot be used to determine the choice – to take Frey's example – between artistic freedom and cultural diversity. These are political questions, it is true, but not ones that can be resolved by referendum. They entail, as it were, meta-questions: about whether, in any case, it is right for the state to engage with culture at all, and if so on what basis. These are political questions of a more fundamental kind than Frey or O'Brien discuss. They are not about what kind of culture be funded, but whether culture be funded at all.

The political argument for music

The general question about whether culture should be funded has long-occupied liberal political theory. The debate is animated by the liberal concern that the state should be neutral as between forms of the good life. This was vividly illustrated in the pages of *Dissent* by an exchange between two leading political philosophers, Ackerman (1999) and Cohen (1999). The two were united by their love of opera, but divided by their views on whether the state should fund it. Ackerman's claim was that, despite the value he places on opera, his tastes have no particular claim on state resources and cannot justify special treatment for opera. Cohen's counter claim is that opera deserves support as culture of high value.

Their debate revisited territory influentially discussed by Dworkin (1985), who like Ackerman was concerned that subsidy for opera was simply a subsidy to the rich and/or those who happen to have a taste or a talent for opera. Dworkin's argument (which I explore in more detail elsewhere, Street 2011) considers the various possible defences of state support, from those of market failure to those of paternalism. He concludes that the only justifiable grounds for publicly funded culture is that it adds 'complexity and depth' (1985, p. 229) and 'diversity and innovation' (1985, p. 231) to the shared language of a community. A similar defence is provided by Brian Barry's *Culture and Equality* (2001), in which he argues that 'excellence' – as opposed to cultural diversity – is the only criterion for the public provision of culture. Neither Dworkin nor Barry furnishes their readers with an account of how 'excellence', or the other qualities that justify public support, are to be discerned.

Keat (2011) has recently revisited these debates, putting them this time in the context of PSB. This time, however, the argument is not about the public funding of opera, but rather of soap opera. He argues, for example, that soap operas serve a democratically valuable role by providing insights into the experience and lives of others. But even though Keat does not follow what some may see as the elitist prejudices of Barry and Dworkin, he too resorts to matters of 'quality' to sustain his case. The argument for PSB provision of soap operas rests on the thought that their quality is higher than that which might be supplied by the commercial market.

So while Dworkin, Barry and Keat, in providing a political rationale for the arts and culture, albeit from different political positions and with different accounts of culture, all share a reliance upon two things: (1) a general assumption about the capacity of culture to do certain things – e.g. to challenge values or enrich language or provide insights; and (2) that there is a clear hierarchy by which we can discriminate between forms of culture and their capacity to perform their cultural function. The implication of their argument is that the judgement rests with those with the expertise to make it. The value of music is to be determined by the cultural elite. This may be no more acceptable than leaving the decision to a technocrat (or a technocrat modified by a referendum).

It is, of course, possible to provide evidence (of a kind) for the quality of publicly provided cultural goods, evidence that depends on more than popular preferences or elite judgements. It can be shown, for instance, that the range of music played by the BBC is much greater than that to be found on commercial radio (Page 2010). Similarly, commercial radio can be shown to be much more conservative than its PSB rivals (Berry and Waldfogel 2001, Baker 2007). In other words, public provision of culture tends to be more diverse, and this can be read as a measure of 'quality'. But there are two problems with this. The first is that this may be a very thin measure of 'diversity', in which the choices and/or differences being measured fall within a narrow spectrum. Critics of the BBC note that while it may play music by many different 'indie' rock artists, it rarely plays either reggae or heavy metal. So the first concern is how the notion of 'diversity' is cashed out in such discussion. Does it constitute real choice? The second (related) problem is that of the value of diversity itself. What value derives from musical diversity; in what ways do listeners benefit from being exposed to musical diversity? The answer to such questions rests upon a claim not just about 'diversity' as such, but rather about music, and the qualities it represents and contains.

Diversity in itself is not to be treasured; or rather, we do not prize diversity or innovation in something which itself is deemed worthless or trivial (e.g. the range of baked beans or breakfast cereals). Diversity of political views is valued because of the alternative conceptions of the good life it provides; and this is valued because of some underlying capacity of human beings to reflect (and act) upon these alternatives in pursuit of some more general good to be realised in this process. Or it is valued because it promotes democracy, and this is deemed valuable in itself. But can we make similar claims for diversity in music? Certainly, the idea that music has value to a society is widespread. See, for example, the argument made by the MP Jesse Norman in his book on the Big Society:

> ... we need to move music, musical performance and singing from the political periphery to a central role as a social and economic, as well as cultural, priority. The research evidence now clearly shows that music confers huge social, cognitive,

emotional and therapeutic benefits, especially on those who take an active part in it. (Norman 2010, n.p.)

The problem with such claims is that they, like others we encountered earlier, regard music as an instrument to the achievement of other social goods, which may as easily be realised by other means. Can music be valued in ways other than its instrumental ability to achieve public goods? Is there intrinsic value to music which can be identified without resort to elite claims about the quality it represents? In the next section, I explore the possibility that such questions can be answered by an approach that sees music as politically constituted.

An alternative approach

So far we have seen the need to avoid arguments that appeal to the unique or ineffable qualities of music. We have also noted the risks of a simple instrumentalism that values music only to the extent that it helps to realise pre-established goals. Equally, we have considered the problems associated with CV and its technocratic implications, and with the elitist assertions of liberal political theorists. The alternative route developed here is one in which we begin by asking how music is constituted politically – how it is given political form and value. This occurs, I want to show, in the political discourses and regulatory regimes in which music features. By examining these closely, we can, I think, see how music is constituted as an object of political value.

This alternative approach focuses on the political value invested in music and the political form given to music, and uses these as the basis from which to understand how policy is to be debated and how it is made. This perspective owes much to Frith's (1996) *Performing Rites*, in which he contends that all engagement with music entails discrimination and judgement, and that these require constructing music as a particular kind of entity. In particular, he argues that aesthetic responses to music encode ethical values – to like a piece of music is not simply to express a taste but an ethical position. A similar approach is adopted by Jane Gaines in her account of how copyright law validates or enshrines a form for creativity. As she writes:

> At the level of Supreme Court rulings and federal statutory developments, the connection between a political goal and an aesthetic form often *appears* to be one of causality. We can almost see forms of culture taking their odd shapes in confirmation of national policy. (Gaines 1991, p. 133, her emphasis)

Both Gaines and Frith suggest that cultural value is constituted by the processes which are applied to it – whether aesthetic judgement or policy-making. My concern here is with the latter.

The political constitution of music

In what follows, I look at court rulings, laws and regulations and at other types of political activity in which music features. My question is simple: what form does music take when it is implicated in political processes of various kinds?

Manifestos and movements

Political movements almost routinely invest music with political meaning and value. From civil rights to the Arab spring, from the Soviet Union to South Africa, from

Rock Against Racism to Live 8, political actors have constituted music as the expression of a vision and a sensibility. The music is understood to speak to the times and experiences in which it is implicated (Eyerman and Jamison 1998, Saul 2003, Clover 2009). And censors and other state agencies have sought to challenge and deny them (Cloonan 1996). But these are just examples of the more obvious forms of music's constitution as a political entity.

More rarely, music is constituted politically in party manifestos; that is, it is deemed worthy of public resources and the policies that distribute those resources. One example of this is Norman's (2010) incorporation of music into the Big Society agenda of the UK Conservative Party that I quoted earlier. Music assumes a very different guise in the manifesto of the Swedish Pirate Party (SPP) whose aim has been to repeal all copyright restrictions upon music. This ambition stems from the party's belief in the idea that music should be free to all:

> Instead of being limited to a cultural canon decided from above, the youths of today have access to the music, theatre and pictures of an entire world. This is something we should embrace, not something we should try to forbid. File sharing is good for society and its people. (Accessed at: http://torrentfreak.com/the-swedish-pirate-party-presents-their-election-manifesto/)

Where Norman constitutes music as a means to social order, the SPP constituted it as a consumer right, one that trumps the claims of artists or the music industries.

The SPP's constitution of music as a consumer right can be contrasted with the music industry's own manifesto, *Liberating Creativity* (UK Music 2010). Music here is constituted as a source of revenue and as a livelihood, albeit glossed by reference to the need for creativity and diversity. Something similar is evident in the European Music Office's (EMO nd) 'Towards a European music policy'. In this, the EMO's Secretary General, Jean-Francois Michel, stresses how music 'above all touches our heart' and how it creates the conditions for 'intercultural dialogue', but how it also generates revenue. So music is constituted both as a commercial product and as a means of attaining 'cultural pluralism'.

These examples, in which music is constituted in one or two dimensions, can be contrasted with *The Manifesto for Music in Scotland*, published by the Royal Society of Edinburgh. In this instance, music assumes a greater political presence than it does in the other cases. In direct echo of the Declaration of Independence, the *Manifesto* announces:

> Humans make music and music makes us human. There are no societies without music and music is the dynamic spirit of a society. Music is what we do together. It is through music that peoples best express and understand themselves.

And on this basis, it argues that:

> The more opportunities there are to make, listen and dance to music the better off we are. The more kinds of music we can make, listen and dance to the better off we are. A nation with a rich musical life will be richer in every other respect. (Frith and Cloonan 2010)

The *Music Manifesto* constitutes music as linked intimately to human flourishing.

What all of these manifestos are doing, however differently, is to stake a claim for music as something other than a mere taste (on a par – in JS Mill's account – with smoking). They are seeking to place it at the heart of a party or policy agenda. This is to represent music as something very different from that which features in CV approaches, and it is to give it a form that is missing from the arguments of the political theorists. Furthermore, it is a process that is not confined to manifestos.

Constitutions

Constitutions – and their interpretations – also act to construct music as a bearer of political value and significance. Anderson (2006) famously referred to the role that national anthems played in the imagining of the national community, but what we might add to this is that some constitutions – in return – accord a formal place to national anthems. Drawing on data from the Comparative Constitutions project (http://www.comparativeconstitutionsproject.org/index.htm), it is possible to identify 99 nations who enshrine the national anthem within them; there are 78 who do not. And of those that make provision for anthems, there are some 70 who also provide for the protection of artists (71%), as compared to those who neither provide for a national anthem or for the protection of artists, 53/78 (68%). These two groups can also be mapped geographically, with Latin America, Southern Europe, Africa, Middle East and Central Europe falling into the first category; and Northern America, Northern Europe, Australia, New Zealand and the Caribbean falling into the latter one.

Establishing music as the object of constitutional provision is but one stage in investing it with political significance. There is also the business of interpreting those constitutions as they apply to music. The First Amendment of the US Constitution was used by the lawyer Chevigny (1991, see also Street 2012) to challenge a New York City ordinance that limited the number of musicians on stage in a night club. The case built upon two particular claims. The first was that 'entertainment', just as much as political speech, was owed constitutional protection. As the Supreme Court stated on a previous occasion: 'Entertainment, as well as political and ideological speech, is protected; motion pictures, programs broadcast by radio and television, and live entertainment, such as musical and dramatic works, fall within the First Amendment' (quoted by Chevigny 1991, p. 108). The second claim that was vital to overturning the New York restrictions was that the *performance* of music, and not just its formal notation, fell within the remit of the First Amendment. What Chevigny (1991) successfully contended was that the overall sound (the arrangement, the range of instruments, etc.) were essential features of the 'expression' to which the Constitution gave protection.

The importance of this case, at least for my argument here, is that the Court gave political weight to the performance and style of music. They established it as equal to, but different from, political speech. They constituted it as a political entity with political worth. Of course, this was the result of a single ruling in a single country (or indeed a single jurisdiction within a country); it does not represent a universal or general ruling on the value of music. What it does represent, however, is how political processes *can act* to invest music with political value, and for that value to be cashed out in public policy – in this case, the abolition of restrictions on the number of musicians allowed to appear on stage and on the styles of music to which an audience had access.

Courts

Such processes, whereby music assumes weight that is accounted for in policy and practice, are also visible in other legal settings. Music has been constituted in a particular form in the criminal courts. One example of this is the 2008 judgement issued by the International Criminal Tribunal for Rwanda (http://www.unhcr.org/cgi-bin/texis/vtx/refworld/rwmain/opendocpdf.pdf?reldoc=y&docid=4935248c2). A song writer, Thomas Bikindi, was accused of using his songs to inspire the atrocities committed by the Hutus in 1994. Although the Tribunal did not find Bikindi guilty on this count (he was imprisoned for 15 years on the basis of other crimes), it did recognise that Bikindi's songs had the capacity to inflame emotions and provoke violence. In other words, the Tribunal made the assumption that songs had the potential to provoke action. Their deliberations gave public form to this thought and, in doing so, invested music with power and value (albeit of a negative or dangerous kind). Something similar was evident in South Africa when the song 'Kill the Boer' was banned, on the grounds that it too could inflame hatred ('South African: ANC orders "Kill the Boer" ban', Daily Telegraph, 7th April 2010).

But the courts do not only invest music with the capacity to cause action. They also assign responsibility for that action. Bikindi was potentially liable because he wrote the songs. They became expressions of views for which he was responsible and which were to be weighed in the balance when he was judged. This too has happened in US and UK courts where defendants have found that the lyrics of rap songs that they have written (and possibly not even recorded) are used as evidence of their state of mind and their intentions. Courts have convicted people of murder on the basis of the sentiments in lyrics scrawled on a sheet of paper (Quinn 2011). There is nothing new in this – the prosecution in the trial of Oscar Wilde used his novel *The Portrait of Dorian Gray* as evidence of his character – but it is illustrative of the way that public bodies act to constitute art (including music) as an entity with mass, as something that causes action, and as a source of responsibility and value.

Intellectual property law

Music does not just acquire value through the interpretations of courts. The law itself constitutes it as a source of value. This is most evident in the law on copyright and intellectual property, where the twin goals of freedom of expression and the right to benefit from one's own creation are resolved – in, for example, extensions to the copyright period; or in the right to parody, where US and UK law differ in the protection they give to parody. The law is also implicated in the question as to whether a 'style', a way of singing or performing, warrants legal protection. Gaines (1991), for instance, analyses the legal exchanges prompted by Nancy Sinatra's claim that she had rights to her style of singing.

Wadlow (2011) makes explicit the politics of the law on copyright in the use of music to brand political organisations. Here, the question is about the ownership of music and the right to limits its political application. The law determines when a political organisation may and may not employ music to communicate its brand or message. He contrasts the case of the British National Party legitimately selling records through its website (even where the artists involved object to being associated in any way with the far right Party), and their music being used without permission and illegally to accompany political advertising.

To get a flavour of what appears to be at stake in such instances, it is worth considering the complaints of the band Chumbawamba, when their song 'Tubthumping' was used by the UK Independence Party (UKIP), without their permission, to convey a sentiment with which the band strongly disagreed. On their website, they wrote:

> Nigel Farage [leader of UKIP] came out at the UKIP conference to our song Tubthumping. If ever there was gross misuse of a band's music this is it. Chumbawamba would like it to go on record that we do not support either David Farrage (*sic*) or UKIP. In fact we would go further and say that David Farrage (*sic*) is an arse, his party is mainly made up of bigots and its policies are racist. Hope that clears up any notion that we in any way approve of use of our song. (Posted at http://www.chumba.com/, 9/9/11)

What the law establishes is whether such complaints are to be accorded force; whether Chumbawamba can have their song removed from UKIP's website. To the extent that the law does or does not act to affect the outcome, it recognises (or denies) rights of ownership and expression in respect of music. It constitutes music in terms of rights of ownership and control; and in doing so, it attributes value to the music and rights to interested parties.

Making law

If the example above illustrates how the interpretation of law leads to the attribution of political form and value to music, then we can see a similar process taking place in the making of law. One instance of this in the UK has been the licensing laws. Although these are often seen (and are presented) as dealing with the sale and consumption of alcohol, they have a direct bearing too on the performance of live music. The reform of the licensing laws of England and Wales in 2003 were widely criticised for the restrictions they imposed on live music. Even if it was not their intention, these laws made it much harder for pubs to host live music. The protests at these changes eventually resulted in reform of the 2003 Act. In one of the debates that led to change in the law, a member of the Upper House of the UK parliament, Lord Redesdale, announced: 'I believe it is a human right to have unamplified music' (Hansard, House of Lords, 4th March 2011, Column 1328). Other peers made similar claims, albeit without resort to the rhetoric of rights. But what they were doing was made explicit in Redesdale's pronouncement: that music could be seen – indeed, should be seen – as the embodiment of rights.

The obverse of this sort of claim is contained in discussion of noise pollution, where the right to silence, to the absence of music that one has not chosen for oneself, is also enshrined in law. And perhaps significantly, noise pollution – unlike other forms of pollution – is understood to be determined, not by some objective scientific measure, by noise levels as experienced by citizens.

Ultimately, all these examples of the political–legal constitution of music can be understood as assigning rights to the performance and reception and distribution of music. What has this to do with policy? In one sense, they are all about what music policy does: constituting music in different ways as the object of policy. But more importantly, this political constitution of music becomes really significant in the attempt to establish a value for music and to weigh it in the balance with other competing policy priorities – in particular, the priorities established by the market vs. priorities established by rights claims.

Music, markets and policy

If the previous section has served to show that music is constituted politically by authoritative actors and institutions of various kinds, this last section shows how this process of political constitution plays into the policy process, and how, in doing so, we return to the question with which I began: how should music be valued? In particular, how should we decide between public support for music as against allowing the market to allocate value? By way of illustration, I consider two examples of policy dilemmas or choices in which the alternatives of regulation or the market are faced. They serve to demonstrate how political evaluation is essential to resolving these dilemmas and choices.

Ofcom and paying for plays

In 2010, Ofcom, the body responsible for regulating telecommunications in the UK, launched a consultation into sponsorship of music radio. This followed a government decision to allow product placement within television. The key question was whether there should be 'integration of commercial communications and programming'. Essentially, this meant the introduction of pay-to-play in order to boost the income streams available to broadcasters. This was not intended as the legitimation of payola; it was essential that any commercial arrangements be transparent to listeners. What it did mean, however, was that tracks could 'be promoted, or sold as products, within programming'; or that a third party could be associated with the 'hit of the hour'; or there could be some kind of financial arrangement in relation to the playlist (Ofcom Broadcasting Code Review, 2010, para 5.39). Ofcom's proposal led to intensive lobbying, in which, on the one side, were advertisers and broadcasters who welcomed the proposals because of what they offered for the commercial viability of radio; on the other side, there were those, most notably UK Music, who saw the reform as threatening music radio's editorial judgement and diversity.

In the end, Ofcom sided with UK Music, concluding that changes to regulations would 'adversely impact on the range and diversity of music played' (Ofcom Broadcasting Code Review, 2010, para 5.55). This policy decision entailed weighing up values in music that would not be revealed either by CV or by some a priori pre-supposition about quality. It entailed the constitution of music as a bearer of value which could be weighed politically in the policy process.

Bruce Springsteen tickets

The idea that music has a value which has to be understood politically is made most explicitly in an argument made by Sandel (2012) in his recent book, *What Money Can't Buy: The Moral Limits of Markets*. In contrast to Dworkin, Barry and Keat, he speaks directly to what it is that we may value in music.

Sandel's overarching concern is with the increasing prevalence of markets (and with the academic and cultural authority of economics as the source of propaganda for marketization). To this extent, he is not disposed to welcome the kind of move made by O'Brien with which I introduced this paper. Sandel argues that the market 'corrupts' the value placed on certain goods (as opposed to commodities) and services, and that it 'crowds out' moral values (Sandel 2012, p. 10). His book is intended to provide the armoury by which to resist the armies of market logic, hell-bent on colonising all aspects of life.

At one point, Sandel's attention turns to the price of tickets for Bruce Springsteen concerts. As is perhaps well known, these are priced considerably below their market value – in Sandel's example $95, compared to $450 for the Stones. This pricing strategy, according to Springsteen (or those who speak for him), is designed to keep tickets within the range of his ordinary (working-class) fans. There are a number of consequences of this, but the one that Sandel focuses upon is the revenue foregone by Springsteen ($4 million per night), and the suggestion that the rock star is offering a 'gift' to his fans. Springsteen is deemed to be challenging the logic of the market, and to be constituting the concert as something more than (or different from) a commercial exchange. Sandel (2012, p. 39) concludes: 'Springsteen may believe, and be right to believe, that to treat his live performance as a purely market good would be to demean it, to value it in the wrong way. In this respect at least, he may have something in common with Pope Benedict'. This last reference is not to Springsteen's deity, but rather to the Pope's objection to tickets for the masses he conducted on a visit to the USA, which were originally distributed for free, being sold for $200. 'Turning sacred goods into instruments of profit', writes Sandel (2012, p. 37), 'values them the wrong way'.

Conclusion

These examples – Ofcom and pay-to-play, and the Springsteen tickets – are instances where there is a tension between the logic of the market for economic efficiency and some countervailing political argument. This is where policy operates. The point is that the challenge posed by politics derives from the political value constituted in music.

Commonly, this value is expressed in terms of rights – which are cashed out in diversity, or freedom of expression, or of ownership. This thought chimes with the argument made by Weintraub (2009, p. 14) in his introduction to a new collection, *Music and Cultural Rights*, where he argues: 'Questions about music as a right bring into focus emergent social relationships among a variety of social actors, including musicians, cultural policy makers, commercial music producers, academics, and activists, among others'. There is very little written on the relationship between music and human and cultural rights; we need more. It will enable us to engage more directly with the question of the value of music, and how this plays into policy-making.

More importantly, it will give us a language by which to establish rival claims to those who wish to consign all cultural policy to the test of CBA and CV. At the same time, it will move beyond the rather abstract and elitist reasoning that political theorists have contributed.

Policy-making about music will still involve hard choices. The arguments will still have an instrumental character, but what is different is how they are resolved. They will not be best resolved through populist referenda or by philosopher kings. Instead, they will be, as they have always been, matters of policy for policy-makers, and for those who can catch the ear of policy-makers. Courts and other actors constitute music as a political entity of substance, and in doing so they help to ground the arguments about the rights that attach to music. But arguments and ideas, important though they are, are not enough. They also require institutions that enable the resolution of conflicts between rights and the market, and that prevent the capitulation to, or cynical instrumentalism of, the neoliberals. And this combination of ideas and institutions is what, I think, makes music policy so interesting; and in the present climate so vital.

Acknowledgements

Work on this article was supported by the ESRC Centre for Competition Policy at the University of East Anglia. Various versions were presented at the 'Policy Notes' Conference in Melbourne, and to research seminars at the Universities of Bergen, East Anglia, Edinburgh, and Leeds. I am very grateful to the many participants, and especially to Shane Homan, Jay Blumler, Matt Brennan, Martin Cloonan, Morten Hviid, David Hesmondhalgh, Torgeir Uberg Naerland and Karin Voltmer.

References

Ackerman, B., 1999. Should opera be subsidized? *Dissent*, 46 (2).
Anderson, B., 2006. *Imagined communities: reflections on the origins and spread of nationalism*. London: Verso.
Baker, E., 2007. *Media concentration and democracy: why ownership matters*. Cambridge: Cambridge University Press.
Barry, B., 2001. *Culture and equality*. Cambridge: Polity.
BBC, 2008. Executive submission to the BBC Trust's review of content and services for younger audiences [online], 16 December. Available at: http://www.bbc.co.uk/bbctrust/assets/files/pdf/regulatory_framework/service_licences/service_reviews/yar/yar_executive.pdf.
BBC Trust, 2011. Radio 1 service licence [online]. London, BBC. Available from: http://www.bbc.co.uk/bbctrust/assets/files/pdf/regulatory_framework/service_licences/radio/2011/radio_one_apr11.pdf.
Berry, S. and Waldfogel, J., 2001. Do mergers increase prioduct variety? Evidence from radio broadcasting. *The quarterly journal of economics*, 116 (3), 1009–1025.
Bostridge, I., 2011. *A singer's notebook*. London: Faber and Faber.
Chevigny, P., 1991. *Gigs: jazz and the cabaret laws in New York City*. New York, NY: Routledge.
Cloonan, M., 1996. *Banned! censorship of popular music in Britain, 1967–1992*. Aldershot: Ashgate.
Clover, J., 2009. *1989: Bob Dylan didn't have this to sing about*. Berkeley, CA: University of California Press.
Cohen, M., 1999. Should opera be subsidized? *Dissent*, 46 (3).
Dworkin, R., 1985. Can a liberal state support art? *In*: R. Dworkin, ed. *A matter of principle*. Cambridge, MA: Harvard University Press, 221–231.
European Music Office (EMO), nd. *Towards a european music policy* [online]. Available from: http://www.emo.org/Publish/document/76/TowardsaEuropeanmusicpolicy.pdf
Eyerman, R. and Jamison, A., 1998. *Music and social movements: mobilizing traditions in the twentieth-century*. Cambridge: Cambridge University Press.
Forde, E., 2012. A tale of two smash hits. *Word*, April, 66–69.
Frey, B., 2003. *Arts and economics*. 2nd ed. Berlin: Springer.
Frith, S., 1996. *Performing rites: on the value of popular music*. Oxford: Oxford University Press.
Frith, S. and Cloonan, M., 2010. *A music manifesto for Scotland*. Edinburgh: Royal Society of Edinburgh.
Gaines, J., 1991. *Contested culture the image, the voice, and the law*. Chapel Hill, NC: University of North Carolina Press.
Keat, R., 2011. Political philosophy and public service broadcasting. *Public reason*, 3 (2), 61–79.

Mill, J.S., 1989/1969. *'On Liberty' and other writings*. Cambridge: Cambridge University Press.

Noonan, D., 2003. Contingent valuation and cultural resources: a meta-analytic review of the literature. *Journal of cultural economics*, 27 (3–4), 159–176.

Norman, J., 2010. *The big society: the anatomy of the new politics*. Buckingham: University of Buckingham Press.

Nussbaum, M., 2001. *Upheavals of thought: the intelligence of emotions*. Cambridge: Cambridge University Press.

O'Brien, D., 2010. *Measuring the value of culture: a report to the department for culture, media and sport* [online]. London, DCMS. Available from: http://www.culture.gov.uk/publications/7660.aspx.

Page, W., 2010. 'A songwriter's perspective on 6Music', *Economic Insight [online]*, PRS for music, Issue 18, 20th May, 1–3. Available at: www.prsformusic.com/economics.

Quinn, E., 2011. 'Taking the rap: violent grime lyrics and the law', paper presented at the *Subcultures, Popular Music and Social Change* conference [online]. London, Metropolitan University. Available from: http://www.londonmet.ac.uk/depts/fass/research/subcultures/.

Sandel, M., 2012. *What money can't buy: the moral limits of markets*. London: Allen Lane.

Saul, S., 2003. *Freedom is, freedom ain't: jazz and the making of the sixties*. Cambridge, MA: Harvard University Press.

Street, J., 2011. The popular, the diverse and the excellent: political values and UK cultural policy. *International journal of cultural policy*, 17 (4), 380–393.

Street, J., 2012. From gigs to giggs: politics, law and live music. *Social semiotics*, 22 (5), 575–585.

UK Music, 2010. *Liberating creativity*. London, UK Music [online]. Available from: http://www.ukmusic.org/policy/liberating-creativity.

Wadlow, C., 2011. The marmite election. *Journal of intellectual property law & practice*, 12 (6), 868–879.

Weintraub, A., 2009. Introduction. *In*: A. Wentraub and B. Yung, eds. *Music and cultural rights*. Chicago, IL: University of Illinois, 1–18.

Willis, E., 2011. *Out of the vinyl deeps*. Minneapolis, MN: University of Minnesota Press.

Irrational amusements, theatre law, and moral reformers in nineteenth-century America: implications for later popular music study

Gillian Margaret Rodger*

University of Wisconsin-Milwaukee, Milwaukee, WI, USA

This paper considers several case studies of conflicts between moral reformers active in US cities and venues catering to working-class audiences from the 1860s to 1880s. For moral reformers, theatrical entertainments, particularly forms with no educational or moral purpose, were deeply corrupting and threatened not only the well-being of the individual, but also that of the nation. These case studies show that tensions emerged when popular styles sought to expand their audience beyond their traditional patrons or to move into respectable areas of the city – in other words, when they did not stay in their traditional place. This is also true of the many hybrid musical forms that combined European-based folk or religious styles with African-American music. Forms such as jazz and rock 'n' roll did not elicit significant protest until they began to find an audience in northern cities among middle- and lower-middle-class youth. Exploring how laws were changed in response to earlier conflicts adds a crucial historical perspective to popular music studies, which tends to remain firmly focused on music from the mid-twentieth century onwards.

The differences between the popular culture of the nineteenth and twentieth centuries seem to be considerable. The technological developments of the late nineteenth century and early twentieth century, such as the phonograph and later radio, film, and television, allowed for the mass mediation of culture in a way that makes the thriving entertainment world of the twentieth century seem quite separate from earlier periods. In addition, the paucity of scholarship on a broad range of nineteenth-century entertainments, has worked against scholars making links between the two centuries until very recently. In this paper, I want to suggest that there are deep and profound links between these worlds, and these can be seen best in persistent themes in the reactions to different forms of popular culture, and efforts to contain or control them. While the USA has never had a formal system of censorship, there have been frequent attempts to eliminate forms of popular culture, or at least to contain them into specific districts.

The most effective means by which performance could be contained in the nineteenth century were through changes to local laws and city ordinances that governed the business dealings of the institutions presenting popular culture to the public. Beginning in the early nineteenth century, lobbying groups were formed to advocate for changes to city ordinances and licensing rules that governed the operations of all legal businesses, and the result was a complex web of interlocking laws relating to the sale of liquor and the presentation of song and dance to the public. In addition, licensing laws contained language relating to indecency and obscenity. Debates over entertainment have continued to the present, and, as a researcher of nineteenth-century entertainment, I have often been struck by the persistence of nineteenth-century logic in contemporary American debates over popular culture.

In this paper, I will begin by exploring a number of nineteenth-century conflicts over the presentation of popular culture in order to show the ways in which moral reform logic came to be firmly embedded in entertainment law. I will also show the ways that conflicts were tied to a range of crises, most notably the many economic failures of the nineteenth century, along with the crisis of the Civil War at mid-century. I will finish by presenting parallels in the reactions to twentieth-century popular music, most notably jazz and rock 'n' roll. While there has been significant change in the culture of the USA in the last two centuries, I want to suggest that it is also worth taking a long view of culture to focus on the elements that have persisted, and to ask how these might change, or at least complicate, the way we view the history of American popular music as they have developed during the twentieth century.

Nineteenth-century theatre law

In nineteenth-century America, laws regulating all forms of amusement were a decidedly local affair. In some cases, laws regulating licensing were enacted at the state level, but often city councils enacted ordinances regulating licensing and building safety. This means that slightly different laws were in place in each region, and sometimes in neighboring towns. While these laws could vary greatly when it came to what forms of leisure were banned, or the penalties assessed to infractions of the law, they did share some common features on the matter of lewd, indecent or disruptive behavior, both on the stage and in the auditorium. In collected volumes of ordinances, laws regulating entertainment tend to be grouped along with other laws regulating other irrational or immoral behaviors. So, for example, theatre licensing laws and excise laws taxing the sale of liquor often appear close together, and along with laws banning prostitution, vagrancy, and Sunday travel. I have found this in every city for which I have consulted state statutes and city ordinances, with the exception of New Orleans, which is distinct from other American cities east of the Mississippi because its laws are based on French Napoleonic Code rather than laws that were derived from English common law that governed the rest of the USA.[1]

This segregation of laws relating to entertainment reflects the views of a significant proportion of the American population towards these activities during the nineteenth century. Despite its thriving entertainment world, nineteenth-century America was famous for its hostility to all forms of theatrical entertainment; these were viewed as having no educational value and were thus considered to be irrational amusements by the devout middle class.[2] Even pioneers like Phineas T. Barnum made only modest inroads in attracting this portion of the population to his apparently education and moral emporium, the American Museum, because of the association between theatrical amusements and vice and sin. In the view of the devout, it was possible for those who were strong enough to resist the temptations such leisure offered and to engage in it sparingly, but a good proportion of the middle-class population avoided the theatre altogether. Despite the success of Museum impresarios like Barnum, urban theatres tended to be the province of the wealthy elite and the working class, and it took most of the nineteenth century for the church-going middle class to be tempted to regularly patronize theatrical entertainment.

Legislators and councilmen, who tended to be members of the urban elite, often found themselves caught between the desire to please their friends and supporters who attended theatres or patronized saloons, and an increasingly organized lobby that sought to severely limit the degrading influence of these amusements, if they could not ban them outright. In the USA, all of the licensing laws I have found forbade indecent or lewd performance, but they were generally hazy about what that entailed, and the enforcement of that portion of the law depended first on someone complaining, and second, on the mayor agreeing that the content was inappropriate. As a result, cases in which theatres were closed were relatively rare, and the theatres targeted tended to be those that were not patronized by the city fathers. This differed greatly from the situation in England, where specific content of dramatic works was regulated as part of the licensing procedure, and the scripts for new works were required to be submitted to a censor's office before they could be performed. In the USA, the propriety of both scripted and improvisatory works were debated at the local level and theatrical performance was subjected to community standards that differed greatly from region to region, city to city, and even town to town.

The differences in standards applied by different regions of the country can be seen in the debate that sprang up around the exhibition of tableaux vivants, or living statues, during the 1840s and 1850s. This form of entertainment, in which acrobats in flesh-colored body stockings re-enacted classical statuary for a paying audience, had come into vogue in Germany in the 1820s. The tableau was a common part of theatrical performance in the eighteenth and early nineteenth century; it was a moment during which the actors and actresses froze in place on the stage at the dramatic climax, or during the finale of an act, in order to let the audience take in the scene as though it was a three-dimensional painting. By the early nineteenth century, these tableaux began to be presented independently of the theatrical work in which they had originated, and they were combined with reenactments of statuary by acrobats, whose training ideally suited them to holding a pose for an extended period. Figure 1 exhibitions of tableaux vivants and living statues began to be staged in the USA in the 1830s for a respectable audience. In many ways, this kind of exhibit could be seen as reflecting the post-revolutionary egalitarian spirit of the new nation, allowing those who lacked the resources to travel to Europe access to the best of European culture. But, by 1840s, complaints about the propriety of these exhibits began to appear in newspapers, and, in large cities such as New York, these displays were coming to be seen as disreputable.

Elsewhere in the country, however, tableaux vivants maintained their status through much of the 1840s but the debates about the decency and propriety of tableaux vivants spread slowly to different regions of the country during that

Figure 1. Unidentified actress dressed in costume for Tableaux Vivant or Living Statue performance, ca. 1870. (Rodger's collection, purchase funded by the Center for twenty first Century Studies, University of Wisconsin-Milwaukee.)

decade, as newspapers picked up stories about these entertainments being protested and banned in east-coast cities. A commentary printed in a New Orleans newspaper in the late 1840s saw the distaste over tableaux vivants as being a sign that northerners were both unnecessarily prudish and unable to appreciate beauty in nature and art:

POPULAR MUSIC AND CULTURAL POLICY

> [Northern newspapers] say the sight of such things is indecent; if that be so, the sight of nearly all the great works of painting and sculpture – pronounced by the united voice of critics of all nations to be master-pieces of genius – is likewise, indecent. It is a sickly prudishness that beholds only the indelicacy of such things – a prudishness that bars all appreciation of the divine beauty evinced in Nature's cunningest work – the human frame, form and face. (Anon 1848a)

Several weeks later, two troupes of model artists were exhibiting themselves in that city, and the *Daily Crescent* praised both for their artistry and skill, noting that there was nothing indecent about the performance. At the same time, the review of Mr. Pinteaux's Model Artists who appeared at the St. Louis Ballroom in the French Quarter, notes that the audience, which was comprised solely of men, had different expectations of the model artists:

> At the St. Louis, when the curtain had fallen upon the last scene of the first part, a most hideous yell was raised by a majority of the gentlemen present. Various screams and howlings, mingled with whistling and cries of the most equivocal character, were thrown in by way of *lagnappe*. This scene lasted through the first tableau of the second part – through its repetition, and during the interval between the first and second tableau, when to the great disgust of those chaste gentlemen, the character again appeared in her proper attire. Here again the cries commenced and lasted until the curtain put an end to the tumult. (Anon 1848b)

This review shows that the problem with tableaux vivants lay not in the content of the staged performance but rather in the reaction of the audience. Commentaries from elsewhere in the USA show that this was not an isolated case, and that tableaux vivants came to be seen as indecent because of the unrestrained and vocal reaction from men in the audience. The hooting and hollering noted by the reviewer made tableaux vivants completely unsuitable for respectable women to attend, and this guaranteed the rapid downward spiral of this entertainment from art to pornography Figures 2 and 3.

Through much of the second half of the nineteenth century, the decency of any theatrical entertainment form was dependent on the presence of respectable middle- and upper-class women in the audience, regardless of what was staged. This increasingly put lower-class entertainment forms into a difficult position because the working-class women they attracted to their audiences were assumed to be prosti- tutes by middle-class moral reformers, who sought, wherever possible, to keep these entertainment forms out of residential areas and away from schools, churches, and other respectable community institutions. One of the most effective mechanisms for achieving this end was in lobbying for changes to city ordinances and licensing rules that governed the operations of all legal businesses.

By the early nineteenth century, large cities in the Northeast of the USA began to write more and more complex laws regulating theatre and other irrational amuse- ments. City governments also worked on laws to regulate the sale of alcohol during the same period, and, in New York, these efforts were not unrelated. The efforts of moral reform societies that were formed to work on specific issues such as temper- ance, vice, prostitution, and poverty were instrumental in driving legislation during the 1820s and 1830s. These organizations not only lobbied government, but also placed editorials in newspapers to garner public support for their efforts. They were also active in finding infractions of the laws for which they had lobbied, and

Figure 2. 'Ballet Group,' these women, who also performed under the name 'The Colonna Troupe,' formed the core of an early Rentz-Santley Burlesque troupe. Stereoview, unknown photographer, ca. 1880. (Rodger's collection.)

making sure that police enforced the new laws by raiding venues, and by initiating legal action to shut venues and impose fines on those breaking the law.[3]

In New York City, the Society for the Reform of Juvenile Delinquents was one of the organizations that came to have an interest in theatrical licensing. This Society, founded in 1824, ran houses of refuge for children whose parents had been committed to the poor house or who had been convicted of criminal acts in the city. Its goal was to train children for employment by placing them in domestic service or in manufacturing positions by the time they were teens so that they could support themselves and live as decent citizens. In 1829, the state legislature approved the appropriation of funds from the New York City Commission of Health to underwrite the costs of this Society, whose governing board was made up of 30 prominent men of the city who were elected and served voluntarily. The appropriated money came from port taxes, which also supported the Mariners' Hospital, and from theatre licensing fees that were paid to the city (State of New York 1835–36, p. 267–271). In 1831, this act was further modified to require a portion of excise taxes be paid to the society, and in 1839, the act was revised to require that all fines

Figure 3. This image of one of the dancers from the Colonna Troupe, possibly Sally Wright who was also known as 'Wiry Sal,' was clearly intended for a male audience. Hand-tinted stereoview, Stereoscopic Gems, ca. 1880. (Rodger's Collection.)

resulting from infractions of theatrical licensing fees be paid to the Society (Edmonds 1863, vol. 5, p. 212–213). Given that the fine for each infraction was $500, the amount of money available to fund the Society's activities was not inconsiderable. In a period of fifteen years, the Society had transformed itself from a charitable organization that was given money by the city to help rehabilitate young people who had become victims to vice or crime, to a society that had an active role and a vested interest in policing theatre law. After the passage of the 1839 Act, part of the Society's activities revolved around theatre visits in the hope of catching managers in infractions of theatre law, and in bringing legal cases against theatre managers in order have fines imposed on them (ibid.).

The timing of the passage of all of these laws and amendments is telling. During the first decades of the nineteenth century, the USA went through a series of minor and major economic recessions. The Society was founded in 1824, shortly after a prolonged depression that ran from 1815 to 1821, and a second, minor recession during 1822–1823. Much of the 1820s were marked by economic decline, which resulted in the increased funding for the society through amendments passed in 1829 and 1831. The final amendment in 1839 came at the beginning of what would become a prolonged and serious depression that ran from 1839 to 1843. Lawmakers, and the general population, were more open to the arguments of moral reformers due to the increased level of anxiety during a period of financial insecurity.

In the nineteenth century, moral reformers argued that personal weakness and failure contributed to national weakness and failure, and in periods when the success of the new nation was in doubt, laws regulating personal morality were seen as a way of ameliorating national crisis. Given that the nation's oldest, largest, and best organized moral reform organizations were based in urban areas, the leaders of these organizations needed to carefully target their campaigns and to push to make the largest gains at times at which their arguments had most sway. They also tended to focus on entertainments that targeted less-wealthy populations; people who were poor were viewed weak and easily led astray, and thus seen as victims of commercial forces such as saloons and theatres that were all too ready to exploit that weakness. Amusements catering to wealthier city residents were generally left untouched, most likely because reformers understood that reforms focused on elite entertainment forms were less likely to win support from legislators.

Legal changes in a time of national unrest: The Civil War

The next period of national crisis occurred during the 1850s, and it came to a height in 1857 with a financial panic, followed by a number of years in which political unrest made the Civil War increasingly inevitable. Variety entertainment, which was a popular theatrical form that had begun as saloon entertainment in the 1840s and continued to expand to a substantial multi-act show comprised of novelties, song, and dance by the 1850s, suffered during the financial panic and many halls closed or scaled back on their performances.[4] By 1859, however, halls offering variety entertainment and alcohol had begun to proliferate as the economy improved, moving from the lower east side of Manhattan and the area surrounding the Bowery, across town to Broadway. This influx of variety halls only increased at the outbreak of the Civil War, when New York became a major mobilizing center for the northern armies.

Broadway had once been the province of the wealthy and elite of the city, and, while this population had moved uptown in the previous decades, they resented the incursion of working-class entertainments into their old neighborhoods and onto the premier shopping street of the city. It took two years of lobbying at the state legislature to effect changes to the theatre licensing laws, and this activity was reflected in a large number of editorials and debates in New York City's newspapers. The arguments most frequently used in opposition to variety were moral ones:

> Within the last six or eight months a class of nuisance has been growing up in some of our principal streets, which demand the immediate and rigorous attention of our police authorities. We refer to the *concert saloons*, as they are called, which abound in Broadway, and which, under guise of singing and selling lager beer, are really the lowest and most infamous houses of prostitution, in which thousands of young men and boys congregate every night, and plunge into the worst excesses of ruinous and disgraceful debauchery. Some of them have licenses for theatrical performances, and resort to petty plays, gymnastic feats, dancing, & c., & c., and an additional means of enticing visitors ... (Anon 1861)

The editorial also criticized the halls for employing 'pretty waiter girls,' who the author declared were really prostitutes, but the most insidious danger of the concert saloons came not from the waiter girls, but from the performances staged at these establishments. The writer continues:

> ... Thousands of young men belonging to respectable families, caught by their advertisements in the *Herald*, are constantly drawn into [the concert saloons], and soon become sunk in debaucheries from which at the outset they would have shrunk with disgust and horror. The plausible cloak of music and theatrical performances blinds the eyes of parents and guardians to the real character of these places, which are thus doing their work of ruin and degradation upon the rapidly increasing number of victims, with perfect impunity and even without suspicion. (ibid.)

Thus, the problem with concert saloons, and variety, was not the entertainment presented on the stage, but in the fundamental debauchery of the form that mixed alcohol and women, who mingled freely with men in the auditorium, encouraging men to indulge in their base instincts. The apparently harmless fun of the entertainment presented, and the location of the halls in proximity to respectable theatres, made this entertainment form even more dangerous to society.

When the new law passed, it was immediately evident that it targeted variety that was staged in concert saloons.[5] In doing so, moral reformers sought not only to protect the patrons of this form, who were predominantly working men of modest means, but also to protect a respectable street from incursions by low-class entertainment forms. Broadway was viewed as 'the most wonderful street in the universe,' and it was the antithesis of the traditional home for the concert saloon, the Bowery (McCabe 1872, p. 123). In the late 1860s, a sensational guidebook to New York described nightlife in the Bowery, including the kinds of entertainment found there:

> At night it is brilliantly illuminated, and the drinking-places are filled by thousands of women, children and men ... These places, open on Sunday, are jammed to suffocation Sunday nights. Actresses too corrupt and dissolute to play anywhere else appear on the boards at the Bowery. Broad farces, indecent comedies, plays of highwaymen, and murderers, are received with shouts by the reeking crowd that fill the low theatres. News-boys, street-sweepers, rag-pickers, begging girls, collectors of cinders, and all who can beg or steal a sixpence, fill the galleries of these corrupt places of amusement. There is not a dance-cellar, a free-and-easy, a concert-saloon, or a vile drinking-place, that presents such a view of the depravity and degradation of New York as the gallery of a Bowery theatre. (Smith 1869, p. 215–216)

Given that concert saloons and other low-class entertainments had long flourished on and around the Bowery with little reaction from New Yorkers, it might seem surprising that the legislature was persuaded to pass a law that specifically targeted these venues. Wealthy citizens did not view low-class entertainment as a problem as long as it stayed in its proper place, out of sight in the poorest parts of the city. The appearance of venues associated with the Bowery on the premier street of the city was what caused outrage. In addition, while the wealthy no longer lived in this part of the city, a number of their favorite theatres were increasingly impinged upon by concert saloons, and the proprietors of these theatres joined with anti-theatrical forces to lobby for a law that worked against the interests of concert saloon managers, arguing that the sidewalks outside their venues were crowded with disreputable people whose presence disrupted their businesses.

The anti-Concert Saloon law, as this law came to be known, sought to eliminate variety by cutting off its major source of revenue – alcohol sales. Initially, police raided theatres of all kinds in New York City to ensure that bar rooms were closed, and it is likely that they did so to show that they did not favor elite populations.

But after this, the energies of the city and the police were focused on variety, and inspections of variety halls came to be a regular part of their yearly licensing renewal. The loss of income did not put variety managers out of business, but rather forced them to innovate. They introduced a door charge and concentrated on presenting a strong show. They also managed to continue to gain from alcohol sales, only now the bar rooms were walled off from the lobby and auditorium and could only be entered from the street. There was, however, nothing to prevent members of the audience getting a pass to leave the auditorium during acts they did not enjoy to exit the theatre and stop into the bar for a beer before returning to the theatre, or heading onto other entertainment. The lack of narrative in variety entertainment made it particularly suitable for intermittent viewing.

Theatre law in the long depression of the 1870s

While the 1862 New York law was passed to protest the mere presence of variety in respectable areas of the city, with little comment on what was actually presented on the stage, the kinds of acts presented increasingly triggered protests in the period after the Civil War. In 1873, the USA was plunged in a deep and prolonged economic depression, which lasted until the end of that decade. This depression caused theatre failures all over the country, and variety managers responded in two different ways. Some theatres sought to expand their audience to cater to women

Figure 4. French Can-can dancer, Saharet, Snap Shot Photo Co., Stereoview Stereoscopic Gems, ca. 1890. (Rodger's Collection.)

and children, as well as their traditional audience of men, and the shows were modified to remove some of the more risqué elements of performance that might offend the new audience. This strand of variety eventually developed into vaudeville, which by the early twentieth century was claiming to be respectable middle-class entertainment.

Figure 5. Clinetop Sisters, dressed for Zouave Drilling, carte de visite, unknown photographer, ca. 1870. (Rodger's Collection.)

The second approach to the economic crash was to offer entertainment that was guaranteed to attract the traditional male audience, and this increasingly revolved around the presentation of the Can-can. The Can–can, a formation dance by a female ballet corps that involved high-kicking choreography, had become popular in New York after it was seen in Offenbach's *La Vie Parisienne* that was staged at the Theatre Français in 1868. The dance quickly became part of the standard choreography of female burlesque troupes, which already included other formation dances and military-style Zouave drills, all performed by scantily clad female dancers Figures 4 and 5. As these troupes attracted more and more opposition, so too did the Can-can, and it became synonymous with indecency when it was presented in low-class venues. While Offenbach's work was revived in March, 1874, and was presented with the Can-can intact by Mlle Aimée's troupe at the Lyceum in New York, when small variety halls began to present the dance during the following summer months – always a slow time for theatres due to the stifling heat of the season – there was a public uproar that initiated a series of police raids that eventually shut down the theatres.[6]

The Can-can and the presence of alcohol in the auditorium were also central to an anti-variety campaign in Cincinnati, Ohio, in the late 1870s. Variety in Cincinnati was severely affected by the economic depression, but as the economy began to improve in the late 1870s, variety halls proliferated in the city. These halls catered to the American, English and Scottish working-class population, who were resident on the west side of Cincinnati, as well as to the sizeable German population, who lived along the city's north edge. The German district was referred to satirically as 'Over-the-Rhine' by the city's English speaking residents because it lay on the north side of the Miami-Erie shipping canal that connected Lake Erie and the Ohio River for barge traffic. The working-class population and the German population were not at all integrated, indeed the working-class residents viewed the Germans with both suspicion and contempt, but in the battles that ensued over entertainment during the late 1870s and early 1880s, they found themselves uniting to fight anti-theatrical forces.

Cincinnati's elite, who lived on the east side of the city, resented the growing number of low-class variety halls and other entertainment venues that proliferated on Vine Street and Race Street. They were less concerned with entertainment in Over-the-Rhine because it was an area of the city that was removed from their homes and businesses, but Vine Street and Race Street lay just two blocks from the area in which elite theatres were located. They were alarmed by the low-class theatres, a number of which staged the Can-can nightly, who ran a thriving business seven days a week. These represented a public nuisance that threatened to drive respectable businesses from two of the city's major commercial thoroughfares. By the late 1870s, tensions had escalated, in part because one of the prominent Cincinnati variety halls, that was located at the top end of the city close to the canal, was locked in a fierce battle with a German variety hall in order to maintain its audience share. As a result, the manager of the hall placed prominent advertising in the English language newspapers, drawing attention to his theatre and to others like it.

The prominence of indecent and low theatrical forms prompted the city's reformers, including the Methodist ministers and reform minded citizens and aldermen, to initiate an attack against variety halls, which they viewed as a blight on one of the city's major thoroughfares. The *Cincinnati Gazette* published a series of commentaries lamenting the decline of the city's theatres, as well as an exposé that described the conditions in most of the city's low-class theatres, including those catering to the German population. As a result, the city aldermen were forced to act.[7] The city council tried to change theatrical licensing laws in order to eliminate variety, or, at the very least, to curtail Sunday performances, but these laws were thwarted on one hand by variety managers, who fought the changes in court and won, but also by the aldermen representing the German residents of the city. These aldermen made sure that the city council did not try to eliminate Sunday beer sales because they understood that the German population would not tolerate them infringing on their leisure, but in doing so, they weakened the ordinance, allowing it to be overturned in the courts.[8]

Despite fighting this battle over the next several years, the Cincinnati city council did not succeed in curtailing variety performances. They did, however, manage to severely disrupt the performances at Thomas Snelbaker's Vine Street Opera House, which was the theatre that had prompted the initial attack. Snelbaker's license was revoked on a number of occasions, and the Can-can performances at his theatre brought so much negative attention to his theatre that he eventually ceased presenting the dance, placing an announcement in the *Cincinnati Commercial* that he intended to present a show that included his Can-can troupe and other 'broad' features in New Orleans (Anon 1879, p. 4). Despite exiling his dancers, his opposition did not stop their attack on his business, but, it took a change of the state laws governing Sunday performances and a gradual shift in audience preferences during the mid-1880s to finally put Snelbaker's theatre and other low-class variety halls out of business.

Similarly, as East Saginaw, Michigan transformed itself from a frontier logging and mill town that attracted thousands of seasonal workers to a respectable city with a varied economic base and a stable residential population, the city's low-class variety hall that offered alcohol, prostitution and burlesque to the city's working men came under attack. During the late 1860s and early 1870s, this city, whose economy relied almost exclusively on processing logs that were cut in the Michigan forest, was home to a broad range of entertainment including several variety theatres, a theatre presenting spoken drama, dance halls, saloons, and brothels. This situation slowly changed during the long depression of the 1870s, and the manager of the Opera House, Warren Bordwell, took over the once-respectable variety hall during this period. He immediately found it was impossible to make a profit on the venue by offering a regular variety show, which was why the previous manager had abandoned the venue and moved across the state to Grand Rapids, a city with a more varied economy. The seasonal nature of employment in Easy Saginaw worked against Bordwell's theatre; in the winter months, which was when most variety was presented, his target audience left town and headed north into the forests to fell trees and to stack them on the frozen river-banks in preparation to sending them downriver for processing in the spring. Before the depression, the former manager of the Opera House had taken his show into the forest, traveling with prostitutes who worked out of a separate tent next to the show tent. But during the depression less wood was required, and indigent working men had less money for leisure, so Bordwell turned to the Can-can and an all-female show to maximize his audience (Rodger 2010, p. 178–189).

It took the town almost twenty years to shut Bordwell's theatre, and he was still fighting the city's ordinance changes in court when he died. Now Saginaw remembers this theatre fondly because it is associated with city's former frontier identity. Given that Saginaw enjoyed economic boom times during the 1850s through the early 1870s, and is now part of the economically failing rust belt of Michigan having been largely abandoned by automobile manufacturing, this nostalgia for a mythical rough and ready past is not surprising. But during the 1880s, town residents were in the process of leaving this frontier identity behind, and they saw the Bordwell's hall, and the entertainment he offered, as being incompatible with the modern city they were creating. Had Bordwell's hall been located on the river-front or near the railroad depot it would have attracted less animosity, because these areas were on the edges of town and peripheral to polite society, but the Opera House was on the main shopping street of East Saginaw, and thus represented a blight and a danger to respectable citizens.

The persistence of nineteenth-century logic into the twentieth century.

These cases show that, in the nineteenth century, both towns and cities were concerned with containing rather than eliminating low-class entertainment. At first, this meant keeping low-class venues separate from venues that catered to polite society. By the 1880s, urban planning had begun to create vice districts within cities. In some cases, like New Orleans, these were districts that hosted brothels and legal prostitution, but in most cities it was the district in which one found entertainment catering to an all male audience, or to working-class, or immigrant, or African-American audiences. This kind of separation could be seen in New York City, for example, as late as the 1980s. Times Square, once the home to respectable commercial theatres had fallen into disrepute and movie houses, strip clubs and burlesque houses continued to operate between shuttered storefronts. Respectable Broadway venues had moved 10 blocks further uptown, and the venues that presented elite art forms – art music, ballet, and the opera – were 10 blocks further north at Lincoln Center. Similarly, Pittsburgh's premier concert hall was on the edge of what had been the vice district that ran along Liberty Avenue between the railroad station and seventh Street. Maps now call this the Cultural District, but when I moved to that city in the early 1990s there was still evidence of the older disreputable theatres in those blocks.

The fact that the segregation of amusements into designated districts continued beyond the end of the nineteenth century suggests that moral reform thinking continued to shape law, custom, and attitudes for a century or more beyond the disappearance or the dissolution of societies that had once been so active in the shaping of laws governing entertainment. This can still sometimes be seen at work in American discourse. Most recently arguments of this kind were part of Rick Santorum's campaign as he vied to become the Republican Presidential candidate.[9] As in the nineteenth century, his rhetoric was most compelling to rural and small-town residents, and to devout, evangelical Christians. While only small portions of the American public continue to subscribe wholesale to the logic of nineteenth-century moral reform, these ideas underlie much of the contemporary law that governs public planning and entertainment, and to some extent they also circulate as 'common sense.' As in the nineteenth century, 'common sense' arguments become most compelling in the face of an apparent crisis, and they continue to be seen in reactions to popular culture, and particularly popular music, throughout the twentieth century.

The electronic mass mediation of popular culture in the early twentieth century through sound recordings, radio, and then television made the containment and segregation of entertainment into specific districts more and more difficult as the century progressed. While local towns had been able to refuse to grant performing licenses to variety, vaudeville, burlesque, minstrelsy, and other popular entertainments that made no educational or moral claims in the nineteenth century, with the advent of radio they could not prevent their residents from tuning into broadcasts from nearby cities. Radio also served to disembody performances. Listeners could hear performances in a range of musical styles knowing nothing about the people playing the music. It also allowed the secret enjoyment of elicit music, so that it was possible to enjoy the new syncopated styles of music that were derived from African-American styles without incurring the social stigma of being seen in public entering the disreputable sections of town to attend performances.

The popularity of ragtime, jazz, and other syncopated music, along with the popular dances of the 1920s, caused consternation all over the country, but the most violent opposition came from small towns, which were also least likely to have jazz venues. For example, the Sioux City, Iowa, *Journal* published a series of anti-jazz articles in the 1920s. Sioux City, which is on the western border between Iowa and Nebraska was a respectable small city. It is far from the Mississippi River, the route by which jazz traveled northwards from New Orleans, and it is more than five hundred miles from Chicago, where there was a thriving jazz scene. 'Is Jungle Music Debasing Society?' one headline screamed, and in a small inset, a headline confirmed 'Voodoo Vitalizes Vice' (Anon 1924, p. 36). While this article is full of violently racist language, the major concern expressed by its author was that jazz music and the venues that played jazz represented a threat to young people that inevitably caused crime, delinquency, and uncontrolled behavior. The article reported that the American Federation of Women's Clubs had launched a national campaign to try and persuade radio stations to cease broadcasting such dangerous music. In other words, they hoped to keep jazz and other syncopated music contained to specific cities and to specific districts within those cities, to which no respectable person would venture.

Similarly, the Sandusky, Ohio, *Register* reported that the city council of Savannah, Georgia, had banned the performance of jazz in that city on 17 April 1922 (Tuttle 1922, p. 1). This article reported that opponents of jazz argued that 'young people needed some restraining measure to keep their morals clean,' and that as a result of these arguments the council had banned 'jazz, syncopated or otherwise, from the stage, [and] from all public dances' and levied a fine of $100 'or 30 days in jail for those who participate in the barred dance or those who permit it at affairs which they control' (ibid.). While this was an extreme case, similar debates, along with dire pronouncements about the degrading influence of this music can be found in American newspapers from small and mid-size cities during this period.

Thirty years later, radio was an old technology and rapidly being surpassed by the new technology of television, which had the advantage of allowing the audience to see the performers and to make judgments about the music accordingly. Swing music and mildly syncopated songs in lush arrangements had become a staple of this new medium. A small number of African-American performers regularly appeared on broadcast variety shows, first on the radio and then later on television, singing this repertoire. Indeed, 1956 saw the advent of the short-lived Nat King

Cole television show; despite persistent protests and the withdrawal of advertisers who underwrote the costs of production, Nat King Cole was able to maintain his presence on NBC for a year before a lack of sponsorship caused the cancelation of his show. If portions of the American audience were not yet ready to watch a well-dressed black man performing the safest of popular repertoire of the period and interacting with white personalities as an equal, they were no more ready to accept newer styles of dance music that were emerging as youth culture in the same period.

The popularity of rock and roll in the 1950s elicited protests that were similar to the reactions to early forms of jazz, although now the opponents understood that they could not completely prevent the broadcast of this music. Instead, they sought to stigmatize the new forms of music, making them socially unacceptable, and they protested loudly enough against dances associated with rock 'n' roll that Elvis's gyrating pelvis could not be shown on television. This censorship was rendered largely ineffective by the delighted screams of the studio audience that signaled the presence of suggestive and illicit choreography just out of camera shot.

Once again, newspaper commentaries on rock 'n' roll used peculiarly nineteenth-century language, describing the music and its associated dances as causing emotional instability, juvenile delinquency, and reflecting the general decline of society (Anon 1956a, 1956b). An article by Dick Reid, from 1960, noted that in its earliest days in the 1940s, rock and roll was the result of musical miscegenation in the poverty of the southern USA (Reid 1960). At the time this article was written, rock 'n' roll was no longer seen as such a threat; by that time more and more urban performers from the north and from California had entered the genre, and acts had become more polished in their musical skills and presentation. Reid observed that jazz had taken a similar path in the 1920s and 1930s as more white musicians began to play it. But in the mid-1950s, local moral reformers sought to keep rock and roll off the airwaves, and communities banned concerts and dances, all in an effort to stop the incursion of the newest low-class music into their respectable middle-class communities.

The negative reaction to rock and roll is generally ascribed to race and the taboo subject of miscegenation, and while these were certainly central in the protests against the form, I want to argue it goes beyond that. The negative reaction to white performers such as Elvis Presley was as much about class and region as it was about a young white man performing music that had earlier been associated exclusively with black performers and audiences, and it was elicited not only by the fear of race mixing, but also by fears that moral weakness would cause the downfall of the nation, which was once again under threat.[10]

It is necessary, I think, to view the reactions to rock 'n' roll in the context of post-war conservatism and anxiety over America's global fight against Communism. Rock and roll emerged in the years after World War II, at the same time as the Red Scare and the Korean War. In this period, personal behavior was once again tied to the well-being of the nation. The HUAC hearings initiated by Senator Joseph McCarthy, resulted in the public questioning of artists, actors, musicians, activists, and scholars – all people who could be written off as non-conformists or as threatening to the status quo. Many of these people were persecuted and lost their ability to work due to blacklisting. Homosexual Americans were also removed from public positions because they were seen as being at risk for blackmail and more susceptible to passing on government secrets and undermining the nation.

In this context, in which personal weakness and criminality were seen as leading not only to personal failure but also to national degradation, rock and roll represented a particularly potent threat. Newspaper commentaries not only made links between rock 'n' roll and anti-social behavior, public violence, promiscuity, and teenage delinquency, they also referred to its hypnotic power over the young people who performed 'primitive' and 'lewd' dances or who succumbed to the cult-like fan behavior associated with performers such as Elvis Presley (Gilbert 1956, p. 11). In a world in which communism was depicted as stripping free thought and individual will from its adherents, rock 'n' roll could be seen as preparing the way for a more serious political and moral threat.[11]

The problem with rock 'n' roll was that it refused to be contained in its original locale. Had it remained a southern regional form, northerners could have felt secure in their sense of superiority over the south. Miscegenation, represented by this hybrid music, could have been safely contained as a southern, 'white trash' problem. Or, had the music moved north, but remained within the African-American communities in northern cities that were racially segregated, it could also have remained contained as a 'black' problem. But once American teenagers in the new suburban areas that had sprung up due to the benefits associated with the GI Bill began to consume this music, there was no way to contain it. This is why the reaction to rock and roll was as strong as it was. As in the nineteenth century, local communities sought to contain this outside threat by banning its performance, but they could no longer ensure that their children had no access to it due to mass mediation, nor could they protect their children from people who did not know their place.

Conclusion

The public debates over popular culture and its public influence continued into the late twentieth century, and very often the language employed to combat new threats had nineteenth-century moral logic at its core. The reaction to rap in the later 1980s was not unlike the reaction to jazz and rock 'n' roll earlier in the twentieth century, and while the protests over songs like NWA's *Fuck the Police* purported to be about the content of the song, they were as much about the presence of music that refused to be contained, breaking into the national music scene.[12] Rap had been present in the African-American music scene since the late 1970s, but when it began to attract audiences from suburban areas, protests were raised.

While some of these links to earlier twentieth century forms of music have been made by popular music scholars, few if any have considered them in light of nineteenth-century logic. I would argue that, given the persistence of this logic into the twenty-first century, it is necessary to consider some of the continuities into the present. Taking a longer view in scholarship allows us to move beyond the tropes of rebellion or resistance that are so often employed in popular culture studies to consider ways in which older forms of social organization continue to be present through the twentieth century in the USA.

To what degree have zoning laws, which continue to be built on an infrastructure of older laws regarding land-use, continued to keep less respectable forms of entertainment, including night clubs, venues catering to the LGBT community, and venues catering exclusively to men, contained in parts of the city to which no decent person would venture? It also gives us a context in which to scrutinize claims that certain forms of music are fundamentally corrupting and represent a threat to decent citizens. Can these campaigns be seen as contemporary versions of the nineteenth-century debates over community standards that occurred in the face of the growing number of touring companies offering sexualized forms of variety and dances like the Can-can? To what extent were campaigns that sought to identify dangerous or threatening music with warning labels, such as that launched by the Parents Music Resource Center in the early 1990s, performing a similar function as the moral reform societies that were so active in the last third of the nineteenth century? Interrogating the logic that underlie these protests and legal frameworks will allow scholars to take a more nuanced view of popular culture as it has developed over the last century or more.

Notes

1. A good summary of the theatrical laws of the USA, dating from the colonial period forward, can be found in Bryan (1993). The first section of this work shows the development of American laws regulating amusements from English common law, the second part examines the development of laws relating to theatre in the USA through specific legal conflicts, and the third part provides texts and major amendments to the theatrical statutes of all of the states up to 1900. In addition to this text, I have examined local municipal ordinances from New York City, Pittsburgh, Philadelphia, Detroit and Saginaw, Michigan, Cincinnati and Columbus, Ohio, New Orleans, Louisiana, and Milwaukee Wisconsin. Despite small differences, the laws governing these cities are not significantly different from those listed in Bryan's work. The major variation tends to lie in the licensing process undergone by theatres in these different cities.

2. While these attitudes differed somewhat by region, the grouping of all laws covering amusements, drinking, and Sunday laws together is reflects their somewhat disreputable status. In the laws listed in Bryan (1993), there are many illustrations of the suspicion with which Americans viewed theatre. For example, Connecticut passed a law entitled 'An Act to prevent theatrical shows and exhibitions' in 1800. Its preamble reads: 'Whereas Theatrical entertainments lead to depravation of manners, and impoverishment of the people ...' (p. 187). In 1877, during a prolonged depression, New Jersey passed a law designed to limit the exhibition of entertainments, viewing them as having 'no good or useful purpose in society' and tending to 'loosen and corrupt the morals of youth' (p. 289). Licensing regulations were stringent in most of the eastern states, and fines for infractions also tended to be high.

3. The municipal archives of the City of New York, for example, holds files for a number of court cases initiated by complaints by moral reform societies. Reading these cases, it is clear that the reformers were sometimes frustrated by the impartiality of the legal system, and that the police and judges did not always share the views of reform societies.

4. For a history of early variety in the USA, see Rodger 2010.

5. 'Chapter 281, An Act to Regulate Places of Amusement in the Cities and Incorporated Villages of this State' (Bryan 1993, p. 299–302). This law required that theatres be licensed as provided in earlier statutes, but in addition it required that no alcohol be available in the theatre auditorium or lobby, and that any saloon within the theatre building be completely walled off and separate from the theatre. Theatre managers were forbidden from holding both a theatrical license and a liquor license and infractions of the law were punishable with a fine of $100–$500 or a prison term of three to twelve months, or both. Inspection of the theatres to insure compliance with the law became part of the yearly license renewal, and all officers of the law were reminded of their duty to enforce the provisions of the law. While many kinds of theatres in New York served alcohol in this period, this legal change disproportionately affected Concert Saloon offering variety because the cost of presenting a large, spectacular show at very low cost was underwritten by alcohol sales. See Rodger (2010, p. 59–71).

POPULAR MUSIC AND CULTURAL POLICY

6. For an extended discussion of the Can-can raids during the summer of 1874, see Rodger (2010, p. 149–155).
7. The Cincinnati *Gazette* ran the expose of variety halls on Monday 11 November 1879, and anti-variety editorials and reports regularly ran in that newspaper between 1878 and 1881.
8. For a longer discussion of the fight over variety in Cincinnati, see Rodger (2010, p. 168–177).
9. The language used by both Rick Santorum and Michele Bachmann during the 2011/12 Republican primary campaign was based on this kind of nineteenth-century moral logic, as was Rick Santorum's speech to the Republican National Convention on 28 August 2012.
10. Elvis Presley performed a particularly potent hybrid music with roots that went back to the early days of both 'race' and 'hillbilly' recording in the southern states during the 1920s. Indeed, Elvis can be seen as continuing the traditions of earlier performers such as Jimmie Rodgers, another native of Mississippi, whose music drew on both the Delta Blues and the jazz traditions of New Orleans, and expressed the experience of rural southerners, black and white alike. Like many of the hillbilly artists of the day, Rodgers was recorded by Ralph Peer during the later 1920s. See http://www.jimmierodgers.com/biography.html (Accessed 3 March 2013, 4:16 pm).
11. It is too easy to forget that the American reaction to communism was also a reaction to atheism. The phrase 'In God We Trust' was added to American coins during the Civil War, another period of crisis, and it first appeared on bank notes in 1957 after the passage of a law by the 84th Congress in 1956. See http://www.treasury.gov/about/education/Pages/in-god-we-trust.aspx (last accessed 12 June12, 9:03 am).
12. Reading protests against this song in the late 1980s and early 1990s, especially in the wake of the 1992 riots, it was very clear that many of the most vocal opponents of the form had not listened to the song, but were reacting to the title. Similarly, rap was most often dismissed as 'not music' but as a dark, 'primitive' and dangerous force in ways that parallel the early reactions to jazz and rock 'n' roll, and also earlier reactions to the threat of the Can-can and low-class performance.

References

Anon., 1848a. *New Orleans Daily Crescent*, 6 March, p. 2.
Anon., 1848b. *New Orleans Daily Crescent*, 25 March, p. 3.
Anon., 1861. *New York Times*, 12 Dec, p. 4.
Anon., 1879. Supplement. *Cincinnati Commercial*, 4 Dec, p. 4.
Anon., 1924. Is jungle music debasing society. *Sioux City [Iowa] Journal*, 10 Aug, p. 36.
Anon., 1956a. Rock-roll madness spreads: more bans. *Oakland Tribune*, 12 July, p. 3.
Anon., 1956b. Rock 'n' roll shows unstability; offers unhealthy release. *Mansfield [Ohio] News-Journal*, 8 Aug, p. 20.
Bryan, George B., 1993. *American theatrical regulation, 1607–1900: conspectus and texts*. Metuchen, NJ: Scarecrow Press.
Edmonds, John W., ed., 1863. An act to create a fund in aid of the society for the reformation of juvenile delinquents in the city of New York, and for other purposes. *In: Statutes at large of the state of New York comprising the revised statutes, as they existed on the 1st day of July, 1862, and all the general public statutes then in force with references to judicial decisions, and the material notes of the revisers in their report to the legislature.* Albany, NY: Weare C. Little/Law Bookseller, Vol. 5, 212–213.
Gilbert, Eugene, 1956. Rock and roll: menace or harmless teenage fun? *Fort Pierce [FL] News Tribune*, 9 Sep, p. 11.
McCabe and James, D., 1872. *Lights and shadows of New York life, or, sights and sensations of the great city.* Philadelphia, PA: National Publishing (Facsimile edition published New York, NY: Farrar, Straus and Giroux, 1970).
Reid, Dick, 1960. Rock and roll: an obituary? *Charleston [WV] Sunday Gazette-Mail*, 15 May, p. 12C.
Rodger, Gillian M., 2010. *Champagne Charlie and pretty Jemima: variety theater in the nineteenth century.* Urbana: University of Illinois Press.

Smith, Matthew Hale, 1869. *Sunshine and shadow in New York*. Hartford, CT: J.B. Burr.

State of New York, 1835–1836. An act to incorporate the society for the reformation of juvenile delinquents in the city of New York. *In: Revised statutes of the state of New York, as altered by the legislature; including the statutory provisions of a general nature, passed from 1828 to 1835 inclusive; with references to judicial decisions: to which are added, certain local acts passed before and since the revised statutes; all the acts of general interest passed during the session of 1836; and an appendix, containing extracts from the original reports of the revisers to the legislature, all the material notes which accompanied those reports, and explanatory remarks*. Albany, NY: Packard and van Benthuysen, Vol. 3, Passed March 29, 1824. Chap. 126, p. 110.

Tuttle, G.W. 1922. Savannah bans jazz as crime. *Sandusky [Ohio] Register*, 19 Apr, p. 1.

Steering a review: some reflections on a gig

Martin Cloonan

Department of Music, University of Glasgow, Glasgow, UK

This article both reports and reflects upon the author's experience as part of the Steering Group on a project which attempted to map the main issues facing the music industries in Scotland. Through analysis of both the research and my role within it, the article seeks to address bigger questions about the role of academics in shaping music policy and suggests that the case study raises questions which resonate far beyond Scotland's borders.

Introduction: a review

I am an academic working in the broad field of Popular Music Studies, and in December 2011, I was invited to join the Steering Group of a project which aimed to review the music sector in Scotland. The research was funded by, and conducted on behalf of, the country's main public funder of the arts, Creative Scotland. It was undertaken to both inform the organisation's music policies and to allow it to gain a greater understanding of both the music sector and what those working within that sector thought Creative Scotland should be doing to help it. This article outlines and reflects upon the work of the Review and raises questions about my own role within it. It falls into six parts. The first explains Creative Scotland's role. The article then outlines the role of Creative Industries Partnerships within Scotland before moving on to discuss the tender for the research work. A discussion of my invitation to join the Steering Group follows. The fifth, and major, part of the article discusses what the Steering Group did, before I conclude with some reflections on the issues which may own role raises for broader academic engagement in shaping music policy.

Creative Scotland

Creative Scotland is a non-departmental public body which was formed in July 2010 via a merger of what was the Scottish Arts Council, the country's main public funder of the arts, with Scottish Screen, its national body for film and television. Three years earlier, responsibility for Scotland's publicly funded national orchestras and its other national companies had been removed from the Scottish Arts Council and located under the direct control of the government. So, the country's major development agency for music (and the arts more broadly) currently does not have oversight of its orchestras and other national companies.[1] However, it is *the* major public funder of the arts in Scotland. In 2010/11 it received a budget of £35.5 m from the Scottish Government for projects which it was allowed to determine for itself and an additional £14.5 m restricted budget for projects which it had to undertake (Creative Scotland 2011a, p. 40). In addition it also distributes funds raised by the UK's National Lottery, set to amount to £19.7 m in 2011/12 and to rise to £28.2 m in 2013/14 as funds diverted to Olympic Games return (ibid.).

In sum, Creative Scotland is a key part of the Scottish arts scene. In common with most publicly funded bodies, it has various objectives and policy statements. This includes a vision:

> That Scotland is recognised as a leading creative nation – one that attracts, develops and retains talent, where the arts and the creative industries are supported and celebrated and their economic contribution fully captured; a nation where the arts and creativity play a central part in the lives, education and well-being of our population. (ibid., p. 5)

In March 2011, Creative Scotland unveiled a 10-year Corporate Plan, *Investing in Scotland's Creative Future*, which included a three-year strategic plan for the cultural sector (Creative Scotland 2011b, p. 1). It had also reviewed its provision for Foundation Organisations which received direct core funding (and accounted for over 50% of its budget), and commenced a review of the flexibly funded organisations which were due to be replaced by a project-based system of Strategic Commissioning from 2013. In addition, Creative Scotland had also committed itself to undertaking sector reviews of its five funded areas – theatre, visual arts, crafts, dance and music – with the aim of developing a complete ecological understanding of the arts sector which identified strengths and gaps (ibid.). These processes have not been without controversy. Creative Scotland has been perceived as not consulting artists enough (BBC 2012) and as being too concerned with the arts' economic, rather than cultural, impact. Its critics included the Scottish Artists Union, which called upon Creative Scotland to 'end business-speak' (see Higgins 2012). Such accusations, combined with a series of attacks from the artistic community, led to the resignation of the organisation's chief executive, Andrew Dixon, in December 2012. Thus, the context of the review of Scotland's music sector was one in which the funder was at the centre of some controversy about its policies. While the research was to remain aloof from this (and it did not form part of the Steering Group's deliberations), it formed an important backdrop to the work, as did some further contexts to which I now turn.

Scottish creative industries partnership

In February 2009, Creative Scotland became part of the Scottish Creative Industries Partnership (SCIP), the aim of which was to bring a number of public agencies with an interest in the arts together. The other bodies included the Scottish Confederation of Local Authorities; the country's two publicly funded economic development agencies, Highlands and Islands Enterprise and Scottish Enterprise; the Scottish Government; the Scottish Funding Council (which funds Further and Higher Education (FE and HE)); and Skills Development Scotland.

In sum, the aim was to include all the major public bodies with an interest in the arts. The organisations chosen for inclusion created a Creative Industries Framework Agreement Implementation Group (CIFAIG), whose job it was to identify gaps in provision and make recommendations about what should be done about them.

The CIFAIG first met in September 2009, and one offshoot from the SCIP project was the setting up a Music Reference Group as one of five such groups across the art forms which Creative Scotland funds. This was established in November 2009 and produced a report in February 2011. Its job was 'to identify growth opportunities and barriers to growth' (Music Reference Group 2011, p. 6). This group produced a report which expressed a desire to grow the sector from a gross valued added total of £230 m in 2011 to £276 m in 2015 (ibid., p. 3), an increase of over 20%. Given the context of the global financial crisis and austerity, this was seen by some commentators as rather ambitious. For example, the Scottish Music Industry Association (SMIA), which is largely drawn from the rock and pop sectors, argued that – given the general state of the economy – managing to stand still would be an achievement (ibid., p. 2).

Thus, the general context was that a relatively new public body, Creative Scotland, was reviewing its provision across the arts and engendering some disquiet from Scotland's artistic community. It was also part of a grouping which was endorsing a growth strategy for the country's music industries which significant parts of those industries felt to be unrealistic. The tender document was also committed to ensuring that these reviews were carried out externally.

A tender

In late November 2011, Creative Scotland issued a tender to undertake its Music Sector Review. According to the tender document, the Review was part of Creative Scotland fulfilling its Corporate Plan and the objectives were as follows:

> To provide an overview of the cultural ecology of music.
>
> To inform our future priorities for investment from existing resources for planning for up to 20% growth by 2014/15.
>
> To provide a basis for the strategic commissioning of external entities to provide service provision which could replace and/or complement existing programmes and services. (Creative Scotland 2011b)

The work was to be in four stages: audit and mapping; analysis; gap analysis and recommendations; and report. The final report was initially envisaged to be with Creative Scotland by the end of May 2012. However, this deadline was to shift significantly. It is worth noting that the fact that the tender was issued in late November, with the bids having to be in by 14 December, suggested that this was not the most open of tenders – something which would have given Creative Scotland's critics more ammunition. I was sent the tender and spoke to colleagues about submitting a bid. However, the timing was not good for those I wished to work with, and while we were keen to do the work, we soon realised that the proposed deadlines were against us.

Meanwhile, the tender document was a little bewildering. Taking each part of what was required in turn, the audit and mapping was meant to describe the sector, note what Creative Scotland supported within it, note local authority support, map 'venues and sales outlets', note festivals and events, summarise existing data, map existing networks and associations, look at 'international engagement', look at 'training provisions at HE and FE', examine capital investment and undertake case studies. The analysis had to include the following: scale, comparative analysis with the UK/Europe, tourism youth, education, the amateur sector, the commercial sector, audiences and participation levels, talent and skills development, touring distribution, venues, Gaelic and languages/traditional arts, equality, engagement and the urban/rural balance. Under this heading those tendering were additionally asked to 'Define Scotland's Distinctive Strengths' via 'positive case studies', identifying where Scotland was a market leader, commenting on music's role in the wider arts ecology, and locating Scotland's music industries within the UK and beyond. The gap analysis had to encompass genres, geography, the roles of agencies and investment. The recommendations had to include what was possible within existing resources and 'if growth were available' (ibid.).[2] What the sources of growth might be remained undefined.

Overall, the tender specification required a lot of work within what was, at least originally, a fairly short space of time. While it was also rather vague in places, it was clear from the tender that the intention was not a mapping in terms of an economic analysis which produced an overall value of the sector, but rather a map of the extent of the music sector which also outlined both its strengths and areas for concern. This was certainly the sort of research which I would usually be interested in. However, having decided not to bid for the research, I was then rather overtaken by events.

An invitation

My background as a researcher within Scotland's music industries is of some significance to what happened next and needs to be explained here. In 2002, I had successfully applied to undertake a mapping exercise which was commissioned by Scotland's main publicly owned economic development agency, Scottish Enterprise (Williamson *et al.* 2003) and was designed to assess the value of the music industry in Scotland.[3] This work was undertaken by myself with fellow academic Simon Frith, and John Williamson, then a sometime academic but also someone well known within the Scottish rock/pop scene and perhaps recently best known in Scotland as manager of Belle and Sebastian for seven years.

The report we were commissioned to undertake was more straightforwardly economic, in the sense that as funders Scottish Enterprise wanted an overall figure for the value of the sector. We have commented previously on what happened to that report (Cloonan *et al.* 2004, Cloonan 2007, p. 131–133) and certainly that experience informs much of what follows. It is sufficient to note here that the *Mapping* report was commissioned just three years after the establishment of the devolved Scottish Parliament, a time when expectations of the new political settlement were high and various interests within the Scottish music industries were jockeying for position within that settlement. This sort of environment was always unlikely to be conducive to widespread acceptance of the sort of non-partisan report to which we aspired. Retrospectively, it is clear to me that we were always likely to ruffle feathers and the report's publication certainly did that. We seemed to upset a lot of people for a variety of reasons – our funders because we didnot explicitly back their policies, and various people within the Scottish music industries who either thought we had under-valued the industry and/or that they did not feature prominently enough in the report. Whatever the 'right' answer to the value of the music industry in Scotland and its attendant issues is, it appeared that the academics had got it wrong.[4]

However, some 10 years later as I contemplated assembling a bid to undertake another mapping exercise, a letter arrived asking me to join the Steering Group for that project. The letter said that Creative Scotland would 'like to draw upon your valuable expertise' (Creative Scotland letter 2 December 2012) – ironically the very thing that had seemingly got us into trouble with our previous report. However, the letter also noted that for those on the Steering Group who were in employment only travel expenses – and not a consultancy fee – were to be paid. Seemingly my expertise was of limited value after all.

My colleague and fellow academic Simon Frith, co-author of the previous mapping report, were sent the same invitation, and we both decided to accept. In part, this can be attributed to the fact that both of us were curious to see what happened, and also intrigued by the fact that sometime pariahs were now being invited to help out. In addition, both Simon and I had continued to develop our interest in music policy. This included holding workshops, funded by the Royal Society of Edinburgh, on music policy, out of which came our own *Music Manifesto for Scotland* (Cloonan and Frith 2011). Presumably we were seen as people with something to say. Moreover we *did* want our research-based work on policy to have an impact and felt a sense of public duty to try and ensure that it did. We also obviously hoped that *this* time we might be listened to.

Following the receipt of various bids, Creative Scotland appointed a consultancy called Ekos to do the work. This company has some specialism in the cultural sector, including having worked on a project assessing the logistics and feasibility of setting up a Scottish Music Industry Association, and another one on the economic value of Scotland's leading music festival, T in the Park.[5] During the Music Review, Ekos were partnered by Nod Knowles, a former Music Officer of the Scottish Arts Council who had just reviewed jazz education in Scotland and had previously worked with Ekos on reviewing Northern Ireland's music sector.[6] As we commenced our tasks, these seemed to be very safe pairs of hands.

A steering group and its meetings

Any analysis of the scope of a music sector soon comments on its complexity and diversity as the range of private and publicly-funded activities, full and part time working practices, small and large enterprises and numerous musical genres are taken into account.[7] Within Scotland, many genres have representative bodies (some have more than one), and within the same genre many people find themselves working with people with whom they are also competing for the same Creative Scotland funds. So one of the problems of providing an overview of a country's music sector is the diversity of interests involved, combined with the competitive nature of the sector. In turn, this raises the question of just how many of those interests can be represented in a Steering Group.

Creative Scotland would not have been unaware of these problems, and initially, in addition to Simon Frith and myself, the Committee comprised of: Caroline Parkinson (one of Creative Scotland's three Directors of Creative Development), Ian Smith (Creative Scotland's Portfolio Manager for Music and Intellectual Property), Martel Ollerenshaw (of the London-based jazz production company, Serious), Stuart Thomas (of the Scottish Music Industry Association),[8] David Francis (from the Traditional Music Forum – a network of 52 traditional music groups – and co-chair of the Scottish Jazz Federation), James Taylor (based in California and Director of ArtistWorks, an education technology company) and Mick Elliott (Chief Executive of the Royal Scottish National Orchestra). It was chaired by Gary West – a member of Creative Scotland's Board and also a traditional musician and piper, who was then Head of the Department of Celtic and Scottish Studies at the University of Edinburgh. This group first met on 19 January 2012 and one of the first tasks it addressed was who else should be added to it. This resulted in the additions of David Scott (University of the West of Scotland and a pop musician) and Peter Honeyman (a musician based at the University of the Highlands and Islands, and leader of its popular music programmes). Implicitly, the criteria were to make the Committee cover the whole musical field, but the end result was that the Committee had a fair smattering of academics of various sorts.

The Committee met under 'Chatham House' rules, whereby it is now possible to report the topics which were discussed and the sorts of things that were said, but not to attribute statements to particular people. My aim here is to give a general flavour of the meetings. The first meeting saw a presentation from Ekos which showed that it was tasked with providing 'an overview of the cultural ecology of music', informing Creative Scotland's future plans and providing 'a basis for strategic commissioning of external entities to address identified priorities'. It was to achieve this by looking at pre-existing information and supplementing this with primary research designed to fill in any gaps. It also promised sector input, which transpired to be primarily done via an online survey and detailed interviews with key personnel.

However, it was apparent in the tender and the presentation that this was *not* a review of how the music industries in Scotland should move forward, but a narrower focus on how Creative Scotland should prioritise its work in music. While the two are related, it was made clear at the first meeting that the project was about where Creative Scotland should sit within the wider music sector. In part, this meant thinking about how Creative Scotland could engage with politicians, but it also meant considering where it could best invest – either by providing more funds for some or by providing different sorts of investment. It was also stressed that Creative Scotland wanted its future developments to be informed by competitiveness and collaborations, and that it was about trying to fund the best that existed while also recognising potential.

The role of the Steering Group was said to be to take part in productive dialogue, act as a sense check and sounding board, be champions for the study and to offer comment and feedback during key stages. It was suggested to us by Creative Scotland that we act as representatives of the Review and that we seek *productive* input from within the industries. This comment may have related to the fate of our previous *Mapping* exercise, of which some within Creative Scotland would have been keenly aware.[9]

The Steering Group was also presented with an outline of what was required in the tender document and details of how the consultants proposed to deal with each requirement. As noted earlier, part of the remit was to define Scotland's 'Distinctive Strengths', with nothing being said about weaknesses, although perhaps this was implicit.

It should also be noted that outside the formal agenda of the meeting, there was a great deal of discussion of the referendum on independence for Scotland, which is to be held in 2014. At the time of the first meeting, the commitment to hold a referendum was the agreed policy of the Scottish Government, and it was making progress in getting the agreement of the UK government to hold the referendum. Such permission was not technically necessary, but attaining it had the potential to make the referendum much more significant. Thus, in political circles, there was a great deal of speculation about the referendum itself and the implications of a 'Yes' vote for independence. Although consideration of the referendum was not part of the consultants' remit, they noted it right at the start of their presentation, where they also noted potential difficulties with the inclusion of the referendum issue in the final report. Nevertheless, this could not remain the 'elephant in the room' and this political backdrop loomed large. Another contextual factor was the cuts which were being made to arts funding across the UK as part of the Coalition government's austerity programme. While not directly impacting on Scottish artists within Scotland (as the Scottish government is funded on a proportionate basis from the UK government's overall budget), any cuts in overall UK government spending would also lead to less spending in Scotland. In addition, cuts in arts funding elsewhere in the UK had obvious potential impact on Scottish acts wishing to, for example, tour England's publicly funded venues. So the first meeting saw the political context looming large as the consultants outlined their intentions.

The second meeting of the Steering Group took place on 13 March 2012. It was presented with some draft questionnaires for various different parties, including one to be sent to local authorities; an online one for the general sector businesses (which was to be advertised in various fora) and another one for individuals. We were also presented with a set of questions which were to be asked during face to face interviews and a list of potential interviewees. Interestingly, in terms of methodology, the consultants had decided here that they would not transcribe interviews but simply take notes. In general, the questionnaires focused on how individuals and/or their businesses were doing and what their view of the sector more generally was. One example of how complex the process of consulting across the music sector is can be gleaned from the fact that the list of possible consultees which was drawn from 30 different organisations/areas of interest.[10] Around 40 interviews were actually planned (some in groups) and participants were assured that responses would be aggregated and non-attributable. Steering Group members were invited to send up to 20 names for consultation. Overall the consultants' intention was to try and build up the most comprehensive picture possible of the sector and the issues it was confronting.

The Steering Group were also shown what desk work the team could do from existing data including that from Creative Scotland, the Scottish Music Centre, reports done for the UK government-funded Youth Music Initiative, the copyright collecting agency PRS for Music and the SMIA, work done by Highlands and

Islands Enterprise on its support mechanisms, details of spending on music by local authorities (from figures from the Chartered Institute of Public Finance and Accountancy), economic data from the Office of National Statistics and the Creative and Cultural Skills training agency and some information on participation from the Scottish Household Survey. There was also information on FE and HE music provision, as well as research undertaken by the UK music industries' representative body, UK Music and various other previous research reports. In short, there was a wide range of information available. However, the assembling of all this information from a variety of sources with various methodologies raised a number of methodological problems which certainly interested us as academics. In particular, most of the information was somewhat piecemeal, and it often included UK-wide figures from which the Scottish figures could only sometimes be extrapolated.

The consultants had also compiled some initial statistics from existing sources (all in the public domain) which suggested that between 6000 and 8000 people were employed in the Scottish music sector. Of these, around 21% were part time and 30% were self-employed. It was found that 81% of Scottish music industries' businesses were staffed by less than five people. Scotland was also held to stand out from the rest of the UK in that the average person spent more on recorded music. Scotland also accounts for 11% of the UK's live music revenue – a figure slightly above the relative size of its population compared to the rest of the UK. It also had a ticketing sector which had expanded by 25% in five years, compared to a UK growth rate of 17% (*Music Week* 25 November 2011, cited by consultants). Another survey reported that around 27% of Scots had been to a pop/rock event in the previous 12 months (Scottish Arts Council 2009).

In education, it was found that eight HE Institutions were offering music programmes to around 1900 students, while in FE 25 Colleges offered courses to around 4800 students. It was soon noted in the meeting that this means that there are around 6700 students being educated in music for a sector which employs no more than 6000 people. Clearly transferable skills were going to be important, as few of these students would go into full time employment in the music sector.

Geographical issues were identified, as a lot of musical activity is concentrated in the Central Belt area, which includes the country's two major cities, Glasgow and Edinburgh. Here, information was patchy and the consultants aimed to get more from the sector and local authorities. A number of other knowledge gaps were identified, including other geographical gaps, some economic data, the overall structure of the industry, the nature of touring, engagement with the international market, details of amateur/community music and details of venues and audiences. In order to fill in these gaps, the surveys outlined above were undertaken. Thus, primary research was to be a key part of this process. In addition, the consultants promised case studies of audience development, industry development, talent development, internationalisation and education. They also promised follow-up discussions and committed themselves to disseminating the final report as widely as possible.

However, within the Steering Group it was striking that of the eight people at this meeting, two were from Creative Scotland and two were the consultants they had commissioned. Of the other four, two were at the Steering Group for the first time. Only two people (including myself) had been at the previous meeting. This may illustrate a perennial problem for steering groups – that of getting regular attendance. However, as my main position is as an academic, and the other person present at both meetings was London-based, the extent to which the Scottish music sector was taking ownership of the project which was being done in its name was clearly questionable.

The next meeting took place on 27 April and began with an update of the research, which included the fact that 210 responses had been received to the questionnaires, 45 interviews had taken place, four more were set and 27 others were being chased. It was emphasised that it was not possible to guarantee representativeness across the sector within the interviews. The consultants went on to outline the good and bad parts of the music sector in Scotland.

The good consisted of the opportunities offered by the online world, more educational opportunities and a more positive attitude within the sector than may have been the case previously. What was not so good was the fragile state of record labels, a lack of agents and managers, a feeling that earnings in the live sector (which, across the UK, had become more valuable than the recording sector),[11] were concentrated towards the top end and a perceived lack of investment in music companies. There were also concerns about cuts in public expenditure at local authority level and questions about the distribution of support from Creative Scotland and others. Interestingly, retention of talent was seen as an issue by some, but not others, suggesting that there was a realisation amongst some in the sector that 'success' might mean leaving the country. There was a long discussion on publishing, where Scotland is not strong, and of the UK-wide Youth Music Initiative, which was generally seen in a positive light and thus as something which needed to continue.[12] Some of the themes said to be emerging included the need to develop entrepreneurship, collaboration with Creative Scotland (and questions about its broader role), the role of the media, questions about who judges quality, the desire for a coherent long term policy and the danger of people simply thinking within their genre group.

The last meeting before the report was due to be received took place on 18 June. Ironically, I was missing this time, as I was presenting an earlier version of this article at the conference in Melbourne which spawned this special edition. I can thus only report on the agenda and copies of the consultants' PowerPoints from the meeting which I received. These show that overall, the sector was held to be healthy and generally felt to be in better shape than when we conducted our mapping exercise (Williamson *et al.* 2003). However, there were concerns that Scotland's festival market was getting flooded, that the country's capital, Edinburgh, lacked suitable mid-size venues (300–900 capacity) and that developing audiences for jazz and new music remained problematic. There also remained questions about where responsibility for developing audiences lay. Gaps in the provision of continuing professional development were also noted. UK-wide cutbacks were seen as impacting in areas such as music services. Concern was also expressed by respondents about the lack of a coherent exports policy. Clarity about Creative Scotland's overall role within music was also called for by some respondents. In sum, the consultants reported emerging issues from their analysis of respondents' views and that they were set to move towards the final report. While the initial timetable was slipping, it was clear that Creative Scotland was rightly placing more emphasis on accuracy than speed.

The draft of the final report was presented to the Steering Group in December 2012, having been presented to Creative Scotland in October. It ran to 116 pages, with six additional pages of suggestions for action and six appendices which spawned another 48 pages. There is not space here to detail all the report's recommendations, but it can be noted that they fell into eight broad categories – music policy, internationalisation, live music, the commerical recording industry, music education and youth music, funding and assessment, people in music, and networks and agencies. It contained little that was new, but much that was sensible, with general themes including calls for better co-ordination of effort, regular meetings of representative bodies, development of coherent policies (especially around internationalisation) and for the collation of better, Scotland-based, statistics.

Overall, there was little too controversial in the report and thus little to disagree with. My main concern was a tactical one. Given the make-up of the Steering Group, my previous experience of the Scottish music industries and of Scottish politics more broadly, I concluded that within the Steering Group it was best for me to try and really push just one issue forward, as this was the best I think could realistically be achieved. There was a need to prioritise. In the broader context of the decline of the recording sector and the increased importance of the live sector, I was convinced that this one issue had to relate to live music. While I was very sympathetic to the call for supporting for Scotland's recording labels which was included in the report, my own experience as a band manager,[13] combined with the fact that, as noted above, the value of live music exceeds that of recorded product in the UK (and, as we showed, did so in Scotland much earlier, see Williamson *et al.* 2003) made me push hard for something to be done to help emerging and lower level bands within live music. In particular, I was keen that some sort of touring circuit across Scotland be organised with the (financial) assistance of Creative Scotland. I was aware that there would be lots of devil in the detail here (and of the potential to upset existing promoters and rival venues to those selected), but had determined that while I might support other proposals within the Steering Group, I would probably only get support for one of my own and this was it.

The meeting which discussed the draft report was highly convivial. Pleasingly, there seemed to be support for my proposal, and it was put to Creative Scotland that they should determine the practicalities. Creative Scotland was also urged to publish and publicise the report, invite comment and then decide its priorities. It was also agreed that the Steering Group could continue to meet as an implementation group. At the time of writing the final report is awaiting publication and it is not clear that the implementation group will come to fruition. However, I remain cautiously optimistic. The Steering Group had witnessed a great deal of goodwill and, despite various differences, there was an overwhelming consensus that the report had got the analysis of a complex sector broadly right and had made suggestions which we could all broadly support. There would be no need for minority reports by dissident voices. But what had my own role been?

Some reflections

My first reflection is that the politics of this review were very different from the *Mapping* which we undertook in 2002. That report took place in the context of the new political settlement (devolution); this one took place when another one (independence) was being mooted. The 2002 research came at a time when much was being sought from the new settlement; this one came at a time when jockeying for position was still evident, but this time mixed with a forward-looking approach which realised that the game may very well be changing and that this was a time for more sober reflection. Not for the first time, the prevailing political atmosphere loomed large over a mapping exercise and the consultants were certainly right to note this early on.

Turning to the research exercise itself, my experience of this and other reports (see Cloonan 2007) are that the most important questions at the start are how the relevant sector is to be defined (where does it begin and end?, see also Hesmondhalgh and Pratt 2005, p. 8–9) and what methodologies are to be adopted (how should it be assessed?). In the latter instance, a welcome mixture of quantitative and qualitative methods was adopted here. However, interviews inevitably involve the tricky question of *who* to talk to, and it is very welcome that around 50 people were spoken to during this research. The decision not to record those interviews may lead to concerns about verification. However, no one was quoted directly in the report and the decision not to record was prompted by a desire to generate more openness on behalf of interviewees. It is hard to judge whether this was successful, but the frankness with which some problems were highlighted suggests that it may well have been.

In terms of my own involvement, there are four things which I would like to address: the involvement of Popular Music Studies academics in policy, why we may be useful, what we should do and what involvement in policy means for Popular Music Studies itself.

For Popular Music Studies academics, a question still remains about whether we should get involved in shaping policy. In the UK, at least there is an imperative to do so as academics are encouraged to ensure that our work has 'impact' and that we engage in knowledge transfer. Despite concerns that I have expressed elsewhere about certain elements within the music industries exhibiting knowledge resistance (Williamson *et al.* 2011), I do think that we can have 'impact'. So do the UK's HE funding councils, whose Research Excellence Framework periodically reviews the research of academic institutions. In the next review, due in 2014, 'impact' will form a key criterion against academics' work which they will be judged.[14] Clearly getting involved in policy is one way where 'impact' can be illustrated and, as Philip Schlesinger (2013, p. 32) has noted apropos the UK, 'the pressure to become a public face is growing inside academia'. It is also clear that academic institutions such as the Manchester Institute of Popular Culture can have 'significant input into cultural policy-making' (Hesmondhalgh and Pratt 2005, p. 12).

However, Holly Kruse (1998) has suggested the need for some caution on the grounds that ultimately, while useful, those Popular Music Studies scholars involved in policy might end up reinforcing existing inequalities. I am not sure that I contributed to that in this work and in many ways my suggestion about touring was an attempt to challenge existing inequalities. I have more sympathy for Edward Said's point that the choice is either to work within the power structure or be powerless (Said 1994, cited Schlesinger 2013, p. 28). Public funding for the arts still has the potential to provide a more level playing field than a simple market-based approach will provide, and in part I saw my role as getting Creative Scotland to think about how it could help overcome existing inequalities. Here, the question is rarely about purely public or private provision, but the appropriate mix. The report showed this, and to me the most obvious need for action was within live music, where the prevailing lack of a touring circuit for emerging acts was clear evidence of market failure.

In the previous article on knowledge resistance alluded to above, John Williamson, myself and Simon Frith (2011) noted that that Popular Music Studies scholars do have options. One is to do the sort of research which parts of the music industries like as it becomes a form of advocacy for their particular world view. Some academics do undertake that sort of work (ibid., p. 470). However, we think it is incumbent upon academics to undertake dispassionate research, not that which has foregone conclusions which suit pre-existing agendas or which advocates the views of a particular private interest. At least some universities allow us enough freedom to mean that 'academics are particularly well placed to make a disinterested contribution to policy' (Schlesinger 2013, p. 33). Another option is simply to remain aloof. While this has some appeal, I assume that this appeal is limited amongst the readers of this journal. Many of us *want* to get involved, so what does that imply?

It has to involve being optimistic, and my optimism here is partly drawn from some things which we outlined in the article concerning why Popular Music Studies scholars might be useful. First, academics have a much longer term view than many people in the music industries. We tend think for longer about issues than many people who have to make quick decisions, so we can provide historical context (ibid., p. 462). Many people in important positions within the music industries do not come from music backgrounds, but from policy backgrounds.[15] They are concerned with the *now* and seldom have time to read history books to get an historical overview of the sector they are working in. Academics not only read history books, some of us actually *write* them. We are therefore ideally placed to say 'hang on a minute, this has happened before, we should learn from that'. In addition, academics' jobs involve keeping up to date with relevant literature and this gives us the potential to provide the sorts of comparative analysis which many the sector cannot.

A related point is that powerful people within the music industries *are* interested in some sorts of academic research, in at least two areas: that research which bolsters their own worldviews, and that which offers such a challenge that they feel that they have to rebut it. We provide examples in our previous articles (Cloonan *et al.* 2004, Williamson *et al.* 2011). More recently further evidence of the need to rebut those who might threaten the status quo came when the former Director of Public Affairs at the BPI,[16] Richard Mollett, attacked the university-based CREATe project as an affront to creators (Mollett 2013). Its sin was to dare to suggest that the UK's copyright system may need reform. Meanwhile, I do not doubt that opportunities to undertake advocacy for parts of the music industries remain.

In addition, academics are (or should be) methodologically rigorous. This means that even if some of those within the music industries don't always like our research they generally know that it can at least be trusted (Frith 2012). We will not simply be partisan or shrink from our findings. As we argued: 'The value of academic work lies precisely in an integrity that necessitates a willingness to tell the bad news as well as the good' (Williamson *et al.* 2011, p. 462). Perhaps, such reasons were behind Simon and I being chosen for the Steering Group. Importantly, we had no sectoral or business axe to grind. The results of the research will be of almost no interest to our employers and will have little, or no, affect on our careers. We did not have to toe the party line of our employers and were perfectly free to pursue what we saw as being the public interest. While it is possible to question our version of the public interest, it is harder to deny that academics are uniquely placed to defend such an interest. Importantly here, we can draw upon those academic standbys of dispassionate and disinterested analysis. As just noted, unlike most other people on the Steering Group I was not there representing a musical genre or industrial sector. I was certainly aware of issues in HE and keen to see that it was not *mis*-represented but I certainly *was not* there representing that sector.

This leads to consideration of the third issue, what academics should do once they are on such steering groups. Frith (2012) sees academics as representatives of the citizen interest and here I agree. Such interests need to go well beyond that simply that of the consumer (Hesmondhalgh and Pratt 2005, p. 12), to embrace the wider social and political field. Earlier Frith, John Williamson and I argued in a joint article that what academics need to do is to produce forms of public knowledge which combine the roles of legislator, interpreter and knowledge provider (Cloonan *et al.* 2004, p. 212). We later suggested that in addition to being public intellectuals academics must have the arrogance of their own expertise, that is, of the particular *forms* of knowledge which we produce, and that academics must be advocates of academic knowledge itself (Williamson *et al.* 2011, p. 471). My determination to push for action within live music was informed not only by experience in the music industries, but also by the fact that Simon and I had been researching that area for three years.[17] I had experienced market failure as a band manager and, as a researcher, could also see its effects historically. I also had the arrogance of my expertise.

But perhaps I was simply giving legitimacy to Creative Scotland and all the policies which it was being criticised for? As noted above, Creative Scotland has certainly a more business-oriented approach than its predecessor and has drawn criticism for this. Perhaps, I was helping to legitimise that. Maybe I was also endorsing its apparently overblown growth targets. But I do not think so. In fact one of the positive things about the Steering Group was how little the furore around Creative Scotland affected our work. The consultants and we just got on with it (with some of us hoping that the furore might actually prove advantageous and deliver things for music which might not otherwise have happened). Meanwhile, I certainly was not performing the sort of advocacy which I have seen in other reports (see Williamson *et al.* 2011). Ultimately much here will depend on what Creative Scotland does with the report and whether it uses an implementation group. Whatever the outcome, I will be free to offer a critique as I do not have a client relationship with the organisation, am not employed by an organisation with an interest in the outcome and have no financial stake in what emerges. Doubtless this may necessitate some deft footwork. As Philip Schlesinger has noted, in such situations: 'To be a critic as well as a kind of insider raises hard questions about whether one can actually ride two horses at once' (Schlesinger 2013, p. 27). Time will tell if I can. Meanwhile Schlesinger's further point that quite often what is at stake is a more complex situation than '"policy" vs. "critique"' (ibid., p. 30) perhaps suggests that it is possible to have a foot in two camps.

Finally, the fact that we were invited and that there was a conference on music policy which led to this special edition suggests something of a sea-change within Popular Music Studies. At its start I think that Popular Music Studies was politically aware, but often not politically *engaged*. Seldom afraid to wear its leftist credentials on its sleeve (Cloonan 2005), Popular Music Studies was also rarely engaged in official politics. A certain political disengagement has come with what might be termed the cultural studies turn in Popular Music Studies where textual analysis has overtaken politics. But in policy analysis and development I see a welcome return to the political within Popular Music Studies. Long may this continue and if nothing else my experience on this gig has convinced me more than ever of the need for Popular Music Studies to remain politically engaged – not for its own sake, but for the music's sake. As has been suggested, dispassionate analysis is necessary and Popular Music Studies scholars are often well placed to both provide it and locate in within a broader historical framework. As I write this, I have no doubt that the real politics of this survey will come post-publication – and I look forward to joining the fray. Providing dispassionate analysis should never preclude being passionate about the outcome.

Notes

1. These are the Royal Scottish National Orchestra, Scottish Opera, Scottish Ballet, the National Theatre of Scotland and the Scottish Chamber Orchestra. For a recent account of their work see Scottish Government (2012).
2. All citations from Creative Scotland (2011b).
3. The phrase the music industry in Scotland was the one we used in this research. However John Williamson and I subsequently developed a model of musical activities which suggests that it is better to think of music industries, plural, rather than a singular music industry. See Williamson and Cloonan (2007).
4. For a flavour of things see Cloonan *et al.* (2004).
5. For more see http://www.ekos-consultants.co.UK/.
6. For more see www.nodknowles.com/.
7. See Cloonan (2007) chapter 4 for some of the problems of previous reports.
8. Thomas was seconded from Creative Scotland to the SMIA. After one meeting he was replaced on the Steering Group by Stewart Henderson, chair of the SMIA.
9. In fact one of the consultants, Nod Knowles, had been Head of Music within the Scottish Arts Council at the time of our *Mapping* report and was interviewed for that report, as was another member of the Steering Group, Ian Smith of Creative Scotland, who was previously regional official for the Musicians' Union in Scotland and had been interviewed in that capacity.
10. Creative Scotland, Scottish Government, Scottish Enterprise, Highlands and Islands Enterprise, SMIA, Scottish Music Centre, MU, Scottish Jazz Federation, Traditional Music, MCPS/PRS, Association of British Orchestras, Feisan nan Gaidheal, Higher Education, Further Education, Composers/Songwriters/Musicians/, Enterprise Music Scotland, Agents/Promoters, labels, Managers, Producers, Publishers/Distributors, Chamber ensembles, National Companies. Youth groups, Making Music Scotland, Piping, the armed forces, brass bands, festivals and venues.
11. See Page and Carey (2009, 2010 and 2011).
12. For details of the Youth Music Initiative in Scotland see www.creativescotland.com/funding/ymi.
13. Between 2006 and 2012 I managed the Glasgow-based band, Zoey Van Goey. See www.zoeyvangoey.com.
14. See www.Ref.ac.uk and Schlesinger (2013, p. 33).
15. For example consider Jo Dipple, who became Chief Executive of UK Music in November 2011 having joined them in 2008 as Senior Policy officer following previously worked in the press and in Downing Street's Communications Unit.
16. The BPI represents the UK's recording sector. See www.bpi.co.uk.
17. See www.gla.ac.UK/schools/cca/research/music/projectsandnetworks/livemusicproject/.

References

BBC, 2012. *Creative Scotland faces criticism from Scottish artists union* [BBC online]. 12 October 2012, Available from: http://www.bbc.co.uk/news/uk-scotland-19932756 [Accessed 22 February 2012].

Cloonan, M., 2005. What is popular music studies? Some observations. *British journal of music education*, 22 (1), 77–93.

Cloonan, M., 2007. *Popular music and the state in the UK*. Aldershot: Ashgate.

Cloonan, M. and Frith, S., 2011. *A music manifesto for Scotland*. Glasgow: Self Published.

Cloonan, M., Williamson, J., and Frith, S., 2004. What is music worth? Some reflections on a Scottish experience. *Popular music*, 23 (2), 205–212.

Creative Industries Music Reference Group, 2011. *Report and Recommendations*. Glasgow: Creative Industries Music Reference Group.

Creative Scotland, 2011a. *Investing in Scotland's creative future: corporate plan 2011–2014*. Edinburgh: Creative Scotland.

Creative Scotland, 2011b. *Procurement for music sector review (tender document)*. Edinburgh: Creative Scotland.

Frith, S., 2012. Introduction to live music exchange. In: *Live music exchange conference*. 4 May 2012, Leeds: Metropolitan University.

Hesmondhalgh, D. and Pratt, A., 2005. Cultural industries and cultural policy. *International journal of cultural policy*, 11 (1), 1–14.

Higgins, C., 2012. Scottish artists lament funding body's 'malaise', *Guardian*, 10 Oct, p. 7.

Kruse, H., 1998. Field of practice: musical production, public policy, and the market. *In*: T. Swiss, J. Sloop, and A. Herman, eds. *Mapping the beat*. Oxford: Blackwell, 187–201.

Mollett, R., 2013. The creative gap. *Bookseller*, 15 Feb, p. 13.

Page, W. and Carey, C., 2009. *Adding up the music industry for 2008*. London: PRS for Music.

Page, W. and Carey, C., 2010. *Adding up the music industry for 2009*. London: PRS for Music.

Page, W. and Carey, C., 2011. *Adding up the music industry for 2010*. London: PRS for Music.

Said, E., 1994. *Representations of the intellectual*. London: Vintage.

Schlesinger, P., 2013. Expertise, the academy and the governance of cultural policy. *Media, culture and society*, 35 (1), 27–35.

Scottish Arts Council, 2009. *Taking part in Scotland 2008*. Edinburgh: Scottish Arts Council.

Scottish Government, 2012. *National performing companies – annual report on activity – 2010/11*. Ediburgh: Scottish Government.

Williamson, J. and Cloonan, M., 2007. Rethinking the music industry. *Popular music*, 26 (2), 305–322.

Williamson, J., Cloonan, M., and Frith, S., 2003. *Mapping the music industry in Scotland: a report for Scottish enterprise*. Glasgow: Scottish Enterprise.

Williamson, J., Cloonan, M., and Frith, S., 2011. Having an impact? Academics, the music industries and the problem of knowledge. *International journal of cultural policy*, 17 (5), 459–474.

Independent creative subcultures and why they matter

Kate Shaw

Melbourne School of Land and Environment, University of Melbourne, Carlton, Melbourne, Australia

Independent creative subcultures, in their various hybrids of music, theatre, art, and new and old media, are the primordial soup of cultural evolution. They have the capacity for a highly definitive influence on their participants – catalysing the transition from consumer to producer for instance – often conferring much broader cultural and social benefit. Creative subcultures make continuing, well-documented, contributions to established city cultures for relatively low outlay. Indie creative activities in particular do not make much money and they do not cost much to set-up. They tend to cluster in areas characterised by low rents and non-residential uses such as retail and industrial areas, but as third wave gentrification reaches into the dark pockets of many cities, cheap rental properties are becoming scarce. This article uses time-series maps of inner Melbourne to show a pattern of tighter and tighter clustering of indie cultural activities as alternative spaces disappear. It looks at where they are going and why, considers the implications of this pattern for the 'creative city', and suggests some policy initiatives to help maintain and nurture independent creative scenes. As Melbourne's live music scene is particularly vulnerable to displacement from increasingly dense and contested inner-urban space, the article focuses on interventions relating to music venues.

Introduction

Independent creative subcultures, in their various hybrids of music, theatre, art, and new and old media, are the primordial soup of cultural evolution. It is within these indie subcultures that the new work begins, often with very low entry thresholds as, unlike other productive activities, participation does not demand much initial skill or experience. Creative subcultures have the capacity for a highly definitive influence on their participants – catalysing the transition from consumer to producer for instance – often conferring much broader cultural and social benefit. The continuing contribution that they make to established city cultures is well documented – an initiative to provide 'breeding places' for collectives of artists and activists in Amsterdam carries the slogan 'No Culture without Subculture' (City of Amsterdam 2003) – often for relatively low outlay.

Indie creative activities in particular do not make much money – they experiment and fail and explore for the fun of it – and they do not cost much to set-up.

The sites of non-profit and low-profit creative activities tend to be clustered in areas characterised by low rents and non-residential uses such as retail and industrial areas, often without the proper permits, where they are unlikely to disturb the neighbours or draw unwanted attention from government planning and building inspectors. But third wave gentrification (Hackworth and Smith 2001) in many cities is reaching into the darker streets and industrial lands, and cheap rental properties are becoming scarce. This article uses time-series maps of inner Melbourne to show a pattern of tighter and tighter clustering of indie cultural activities as alternative spaces disappear. It looks at where they are going and why, and considers the implications of this pattern for the 'creative city'. Finally, the article proposes some policy and planning reforms that, with relatively small government effort, would help maintain existing and nurture new independent creative subcultures.

On indie subcultures

Notwithstanding the often rapid incorporation of their products into the mainstream, all indie subcultures begin, by definition, in opposition to the dominant, commercial culture. Dick Hebdige, in his seminal work *Subculture: The Meaning of Style* (1979) sees subcultures in general as 'symbolic forms of resistance' (p. 80). Indie creative subcultures are characterised by the difference from the mainstream in their music and art, and by the alternative politics that roam and redefine the edges of the dominant culture. They are countercultural, what used to be called the avant-garde: 'innovative, experimental, challenging and devoted to the overthrow of orthodoxies' (McAuliffe 2004, p. 103).

Indie subcultures are self-consciously marginal. They are first and foremost social groups in the sense defined by Young (1990) as 'collective[s] of people who have affinity with one another because of a set of practices or way of life; they differentiate themselves from or are differentiated by at least one other group according to these cultural forms' (p. 186). 'Near the core of the radical project is the artist', says Ley (1996, p. 188), and it is true that music and artistic subcultures have at their centre an alternative politics. Alternative cultures took clear form in the 1960s across the Western world, but they have an ancestry that can be traced back to Africa and the black roots of the American South (Hebdige 1979), to the dadaists and surrealists of early-twentieth-century Europe, to the existentialists in Paris in the 1940s and 1950s and later the situationists amongst other tangled strands (Marcus 1989). All contain elements of resistance, subversion, anti-establishment or anti-'art', deliberately defying reason or control, questioning and challenging. In his Secret History of the Twentieth Century, *Lipstick Traces*, Greil Marcus points out that the lineage of alternative culture is complex, as 'every new manifestation in culture rewrites the past':

> but in all times forgotten actors emerge from the past not as ancestors but as familiars. In the 1920s in literary America it was Herman Melville; in the rock 'n' roll 1960s it was Mississippi bluesman Robert Johnson of the 1930s; in the entropic Western 1970s it was the carefully absolutist German critic Walter Benjamin of the 1920s and 1930s. In 1976 and 1977, and in the years to follow, as symbolically remade by the Sex Pistols, it was, perhaps, dadaists, lettrists, situationists, and various medieval heretics. (Marcus 1989, p. 21–22)

De Botton (2004) draws similar links when discussing bohemia in the proper sense:

> One can wind the word around a number of different artistic and social phenomena of the last two hundred years, from Romanticism to Surrealism, from the Beatniks to the Punks, from the Situationists to the Kibbutzniks, and still not snap a thread binding something important together. (p. 277–278)

These threads continue unbroken; perhaps they are even thickening. Punk knowingly drew on blues and the situationists (Marcus 1989); new wave, neo-punk, post-punk, garage rock, alt rock and grunge acknowledge their political antecedents and each other in their sound, style and reasoning, referencing so many of their ancestors that the fusions and new forms they produce are infinite. If there is a single binding theme it is a rejection of mass-produced, commercialised culture.

The concept of the indie scene has thickened too, to include not only all the arrangements of proponents, participants, audiences, supports and infrastructures involved in the production of creative subculture, but the connections between particular forms (writing, music, theatre, art, film etc.). Geoff Stahl, following Straw (1991), uses the idea of the scene to refer to the 'extensive inter-related networks, circuits and alliances formed both inside and outside the city', allowing a description of the 'many resources marshalled together to support cultural activity in the city' (Stahl 2004, p. 54). He proposes further that over time, 'any scene becomes spatially embedded according to a dense array of social, industrial and institutional infrastructures, all of which operate at a local and trans-local level' (ibid.).

Scene carries a fundamental association with place. Stahl argues in relation to the indie music scene that 'where bands come from and where they produce their music are significant aspects of how they register in the imaginations of fans and other music-makers':

> ... the Olympia scene, the Seattle scene, the Dunedin scene and the Manchester scene are all signifiers that draw explicit links between the urban referent and images of a vibrant subcultural hub. Spatially coded in this way, city-as-sign and city-as-scene are often conflated in a manner that privileges an aesthetic experience of, and commitment to, the city. Indie bands and their music are understood by fans and artists alike to be deeply connected with specific places, a sign of their unwavering allegiance to an ideology of small-scale production, a deep sense of commitment to their region's underground, and an awareness of their role as bearers of its subterranean values, which takes the form of (an often ironic ...) civic boosterism. (Stahl 2004, p. 55)

The argument applies to other artforms: the Melbourne street art and independent theatre scenes are as closely associated with the city as its internationally recognised live music scene. It is the complex relationship between indie subcultures, the low thresholds they have to entry, and the places in which they locate that forms the basis of this article.

On the Melbourne indie scene

One of my favourite stories about creative subcultures and low thresholds is told by Rose Chong (personal communication, 2010) – a costume designer and Melbourne legend. Rose arrived in Melbourne in the early 1970s and through a friend who was a student at Melbourne University wandered one day into the nearby Pram

Factory in Carlton. The Pram Factory was the home of Melbourne's first independent theatre collective, the Australian Performing Group (APG). In the words of John Timlin:

> The Pram Factory is a focal point of much of Carlton's intellectual, artistic and political life. A refugee camp, housing dissidents of various political, theatrical and social complexion who find within its walls an attempt to forge a working structure which can effectively deal with the problems of theatre without the oppressions of hierarchical organization. In the beginning it was a loose assemblage of people most of whom emanated from the Melbourne University campus. The emphasis was theatrical rather than political though this was later to change … It was a rough and tough group, heavily iconoclastic and united in its contempt for theatres like The Old Tote and The Melbourne Theatre Company whose consistent programming of plays derived from Broadway and the West End typified the cultural cringe then endemic in this country. … Structurally, in terms of organisation, the APG described itself as a 'democratic collective of actors, writers, designers etc.' It was, in the accepted wisdom of those days, one person, one vote. All shared in the programming; roles were multi-functional – writers could act, actors write, administrators build the set. … Drama is a communal art. It needs writers and actors and technicians and ticket sellers and designers and painters of walls. Without each other, not one of these people would be meaningful. In so far as the APG is an alternative, it is so because its political form is such as to give each person a share in deciding what affects another. It is frightening to each of us at different levels, for different reasons but, for those of us who choose to remain, it is the best way to work; trust is the only way in which the theatre can take those risks necessary to create something new. (2006 cited in Ingleton 2006)

Rose Chong was hanging around the Pram Factory when someone asked if she could sew. She could, and began making costumes for APG plays, and then for Australia's first independent film, *Dimboola*, and as her practice expanded, she bought a shop in Gertrude Street, Fitzroy. Gertrude Street was one of the meanest streets of the time, full of rough pubs and vacant shops and cheap rents, and was the subject of many powerful songs from Archie Roach – an Indigenous singer–songwriter and legend in his own right, who lived much of his life in the area (see Shaw 2009). Rose settled there because it was 'dirt cheap and no-one else wanted it', to become one of Melbourne's most accessible and quirky costume design businesses.

Many of Melbourne's best-known actors, writers, designers and musicians found their medium in the APG. Max Gillies, Peter Cummins, Bruce Spence, John Romeril, Bill Garner, Helen Garner, Daniel Keene, Barry Dickins, Sue Ingleton, Peter Corrigan, Evelyn Krape and Jane Clifton made the transition into Melbourne's mainstream from the APG. Others, including Lindzee Smith and Phil Motherwell, lingered on the edges, feeding the next generations of writers and musicians from Nick Cave to MKA's (Theatre of New Writing) Toby Manderson-Galvin. Betty Burstall formed the Pram Factory's stable mate, La Mama Theatre, around the corner, and Jon Hawkes founded Circus Oz, both of which continue today:

> The Australian Performing Group was an agent of change and, some thirty years after its demise, its seminal influence on the cultural life of Australia is at last recognised. It stimulated a whole generation to see themselves in a new light, to see their culture emerge as truly Australian and to claim it thus. From the creative community that was the Pram Factory came many gifted writers and actors, directors of film, theatre and TV, artists, musicians and singers, circus performers, arts administrators and community artists. It is unique in the history of the arts in Australia, maybe in the

world. It was very much of its time, and was at the cutting edge of theatre, new left politics, comedy, popular theatre, new Australian writing, puppetry and of course, circus. Circus Oz remains the last, great living branch of the Pram Factory tree. (Williams 2006, cited in Ingleton 2006)

Dr Jean Battersby of the Australia Council of the Arts, 1970–1971, said in *The Age* at the time of the Pram Factory and La Mama receiving their first significant government funds ($9000 for the APG and $5000 for La Mama) that:

> These two theatres are doing the most experimental work. It's absolutely vital to support experimental work. Unless you get people experimenting now you won't get your great classics in a hundred years time. When you are supporting experiments in anything, you must be prepared for a great deal of wastage, you might support a hundred plays before you get a great play. (cited in Ingleton 2006)

The great cross-medium collaborations continued: John Romeril with Paul Kelly with Archie Roach and Ruby Hunter; Nick Cave with Richard Lowenstein, Sam Sejavka, Michael Hutchence; writers, musicians, actors, directors, often changing roles and all expressing a distinctive Melbourne identity and sense of place. Many years after the closing of the Pram Factory, Paul Kelly spoke at a rally to support Australian live music and stressed the importance of having the places to play:

> I came to Melbourne in 1977 and started playing in small pubs in the inner city. ... You don't learn how to write a song at school, you don't do a TAFE course in how to play in front of an audience. These places were my universities. (Kelly 2010)

Some of the great institutions continue too: along with La Mama and Circus Oz, the independent Astor cinema, Gertrude Contemporary Gallery and the much-loved live music venues the Tote Hotel in Collingwood, the Corner Hotel in Richmond and the Esplanade Hotel in St. Kilda, which itself has been home to multi-media collaborations involving live music, visual art, film and TV and various kinds of performance for many decades, and of which a local comedian said recently:

> I often have breakfast at the Espy in St. Kilda. The Espy used to have Sunday-after-noon stand-up, which is where I first saw live comedy and got inspired to try it myself. Somehow I've made a living out of it for 20 years, but no one really knows who the hell I am. (Hardy 2012)

But these places are occupying increasingly valuable real estate, and the small theatres and dingy back rooms and beer gardens of pubs where people can walk in, get inspired, try out and make a lot of noise, are under pressure from the raft of issues that affect gentrifying cities the world over.

On the place of indie subcultures

Indie scenes need centrality for interaction and they need cheap space. In the last 20 years in particular, in the global third wave of gentrification (Hackworth and Smith 2001), under-capitalised sites in inner cities have become key targets for redevelopment and regeneration and spaces not put to highest and best economic use are becoming harder to find. A further threat to indie subcultures exists in the new concentrations and reach of corporate ownership, where 'corporate control in the urban environment and night-life economies is further usurping and commercialising public space, segmenting and gentrifying markets and marginalising alternative and creative local development' (Hollands and Chatterton 2003, p. 361).

The marginality of indie subcultures and their activities has long ensured their lack of formal recognition, indeed, the antagonistic relationship between the indie scene and the dominant culture is a defining feature. But this relationship is changing. For participants in indie scenes, the threat to their place in the city is such that they have little room to move. Defined by images of opposition, and self-consciously marginal, they are faced with the invidious options of standing up for their place or being moved on (see Shaw 2005 for a discussion of this phenomenon).

Participants in indie subcultures are not always marginal in class terms, but they are usually economically marginal and under powerful pressure to conform to the dominant culture. Through constraining cultural policies and funding arrangements, inequitable planning practices and inadequate provision of affordable housing and work and performance spaces, the locational options for participants in the indie scene are declining. The threat to their place in the city has produced mobilisations in many parts of the world, often based explicitly on the claim to their right to the city.

At the same time, the pressure on city governments to support local culture is heightened with the increasing symbolic value of cultural diversity. The economic benefits of 'creativity' have spawned an industry of consultants on how best to build cultural capital (Bianchini 1995, Landry 2000, Florida 2002, Montgomery 2004). Their advice is usually on how to attract the corporate headquarters, tourists and middle class residents whose locational decisions are based on the qualities of place (all other factors being equal) and whose options are rapidly expanding. Local cultural scenes, whilst not essential to the 'creative city' ('culture' can be bought in), are being used to great effect in city place-marketing campaigns.

As with the currently popular strategies of 'culture-led regeneration' (Porter and Shaw 2009), however, the emphasis on arts and culture to boost the local economy creates a paradox. Not only does the attraction of new investors and consumers often require substantial state expenditure that is oriented more to the new businesses and tourists than long-term locals, but the success of the strategy is premised on increasing land prices and rents, driving out marginal cultural producers and destroying what genuine diversity the city had in the first instance. It is a familiar contradiction: David Harvey observed two decades ago that much of this kind of 'postmodern production ... is precisely about the selling of place as part and parcel of an ever-deepening commodity culture. The result is that places that seek to differentiate themselves end up creating a kind of serial replication of homogeneity' (Harvey 1993, p. 8).

On the 'creative city'

The contemporary global preoccupation with the creative city throws this contradiction into sharp relief. The idea of the city as creative, innovative, a meeting place for the exchange of goods and knowledge, has been around for centuries. People have been travelling to cities for work and human contact since cities began.

But 10 years ago an American economics professor reversed that analysis with the proposition that it is the jobs that follow the people – that is, that the corporate headquarters want to be where the 'creative class' is – and that any city wanting to attract high-end business should concentrate on attracting the 'creative class'. Florida's (2002) creative class consists of urban professionals in the arts and entertainment industries, IT, education, business, law and finance, the main criterion for membership apparently being white-collar salary-earning capacity. This class has been theorised in other ways: in 1984[1979] Bourdieu called it the 'new petite bourgeoisie', and in 1993, the 'dominant class'. It is Ley's (1996) 'new middle class', Brooks' (2000) 'new upper class' or, as he calls its members, 'bobos' (bourgeois bohemians). Smith (2002) called them gentrifiers. McGuigan (2009) suggests they are what would 'otherwise be called routinely the professional-managerial class' (p. 293) – the inner and middle-suburban denizens that the Australian media know as the 'AB demographic', being high in both cultural and financial capital.

Florida's (2002) *The Rise of the Creative Class* and league tables of more and less creative cities sent city governments all over the world into a competitive scramble for well-paid professionals from somewhere else, mainly through providing the cultural infrastructure, bike paths, al fresco dining, small bars and general authenticity that the creative class apparently desires. The creative city-inspired urban renewal strategies that accompany these efforts (Porter and Shaw 2009) have been analysed over the last decade by a range of theorists and commentators, many of whom conclude that they mostly do not work (e.g. Malanga 2004, Berry 2005, Kotkin 2005, Peck 2005, Vicario and Martinez Monje 2005, Shaw 2006, Atkinson and Easthope 2009). That is, they tend not to attract the footloose global elite unless the hard infrastructure is installed too – the starchitect-designed galleries, convention centres, luxury hotels, office buildings and car parks – which makes it look rather like neoliberal development-as-usual. Most creative city strategies are indeed economic development strategies which – if they are successful – become gentrification strategies. Their success is measured in terms of decreasing vacancy rates and increasing rents – anathema to the fundamentals of the independent creative subcultures that feed city cultures everywhere.

Creative city strategies do not easily accommodate practising artists. The national government arts funding body, the Australia Council for the Arts, has found that the relative financial disadvantage of practicing artists – musicians, composers and songwriters, visual artists and craft practitioners, actors, directors, dancers and choreographers, writers and community cultural development workers – has worsened over the past 20 years (Throsby and Zednik 2010). In the Australia Council report, *Do you really expect to get paid?* Throsby and Zednik find that a very few artists in Australia earn high incomes and that most earn very low incomes. More than half Australia's artists have a creative income of less than AU $10,000 a year. Only 12% of artists earned more than $50,000 from their art in the 2007–2008 financial year:

> Even when other arts-related earnings and non-arts income are added in, the gross incomes of artists, from which they must finance their professional practice as well as the demands of everyday living, are substantially less than managerial and professional earnings. Indeed their total incomes on average are lower than those of all occupational groups, including non-professional and blue-collar occupations. (Throsby and Zednik 2010, p. 9)

Porter and Shaw's (2009) collection of stories of urban regeneration strategies throughout the world provides little reason to conclude it is much different elsewhere. The loss of cheap space to live and work and display and perform is creating very real tensions. The particular problem for cities that want economic development and cultural vitality is that one tends to occur at the expense of the other. This poses a dilemma for advocates of a genuinely creative city. For the many artists who make it out of the primordial soup and into fine careers, their art is often their salvation. For cities too, a fine local culture depends on healthy creative subcultures, and builds on local strengths. As a counterpoint to importing global strategies designed to bring in a 'creative class' from elsewhere, the larger research project from which this article is drawn examined the practices and locations of local creative subcultures in Melbourne's already powerful indie scene. The object was to identify where the indie subcultures are in gentrifying Melbourne and why they are where they are, with the intent of determining the implications for city planning. The next section of this article discusses the methods used in the research, and shows where indie subcultures in Melbourne are locating.

On the method

Cultural activities in Melbourne were mapped over a period of 20 years at five-year intervals correlating with the Australian census years. They begin in 1991 and conclude in 2009 – a final map in 2011 was intended but not possible because of a shortfall in the funding received from the Australian Research Council. The key media selected were live music, theatre/performing arts, visual arts and crafts and film/screenings. Part of the reasoning for choosing these media is that they all advertise for audiences and therefore have searchable records of their events; in addition, the information provided in the advertisements allows an assessment of the formality of the medium (commercial, community-based, or independent). The sites of the activities were drawn from archival and contemporary listings: gig guides, theatre guides, gallery guides and film listings, in all the hardcopy mainstream, indie and street media available (albeit in different incarnations) throughout the 20-year period.

In classifying cultural activities as commercial, community or indie, the guiding principle was that these essentially differ in how profit-oriented the set-up for the activities was. There are five main sources of funding for arts-oriented activities:

- public funding, which includes long-term subsidies and project grants from funding bodies in all levels of government, and usually requires accountable acquittal of funds or programming requirements;
- private donations and benefactors, mainly endowments by private individuals or institutions, and corporate sponsors;
- commercial profit (which includes sales, box office takings, subscriptions, sales of related products and merchandise, and advertising);
- cross-subsidy, in which the profits from one activity are funnelled into another, loss-making one;
- 'gift economy', which includes donations in kind, time, work, expertise, space, transport, technical know-how, and which the donors may expect to recover later, again in kind (publicity, social capital, skills, reciprocated volunteer work, etc.).

Table 1. Sources of income.

Source of income Formality	External Commercial sales	External Public subsidy	External private donation/ sponsorships	Internal trusts/ collective self-funding	Artist 'gift economy'	Artist Cross- subsidy
Community	X	MAIN	X	MAIN	X	X
Indie	X	X	X	X	X	X
Commercial	MAIN	NO	X	NO	NO	NO

Table 2. Assessment of formality.

Formality	Curatorial policy
Community	Members of a group OR art important for the group (identity/culture)
Indie	Quality OR style of work
Commercial	Mainly business-oriented (profitable) AND venues for hire

These are not mutually exclusive, but are resorted to in different measures in order to cover the costs of artistic production (Table 1).

The fundamental dividing principle is that 'commercial' activities are essentially profit-oriented, and would not exist if they were consistently making a loss – this is artistic production fully embedded in the market economy, in which art is a mode of entertainment. 'Indie' activities might be sporadically profitable, but would accept financial losses – placing them in a hybrid position on the periphery of market capitalism, selectively engaged and disengaged from its workings. 'Community' activities are to a high degree exempt from market logic, because they receive sufficient public or private funding, are engaged in non-profit activities or present the artistic works by the members of their own community with community-building goals (Table 2).

Since we were mapping music venues, theatres, studios or shops and cinemas – that is the sites of the activity, rather than trying to list bands, plays, artists and films – we identified curatorial policies that match each business model, and if it was not obvious, gauged it from band line-ups, language used in publicity materials, observing the clientele and if necessary, informal interviews with the staff. Wherever possible we avoided taste-based judgement, in which indie status would be awarded only to 'edgy' or 'cool' artworks and artforms.

The logic of profitability and curatorial policy is slightly different in each category:

- in MUSIC, most venues and events are commercially viable (as they tend to derive their profit from liquor sales); therefore, we focused on the bands and artists programmed. Since music venues do not bear the production costs of the music they programme and are likely to make a profit even if the band makes a loss, an 'indie' venue had to show consistent support of independent music in order to qualify (this entailed indie artists programmed on Friday and Saturday nights or occupying at least 50% of the total programming space or consistent support of niche tastes, such as heavy metal or progressive electronic music). As music is rarely publicly subsidised, 'community' venues are comparatively few in number and generally specialise in classical music or traditional music as part of community festivals (e.g. Melbourne Recital Centre and community arts centres).

- PERFORMING ARTS are labour-intensive, expensive to produce, and very rarely commercially viable. Only the large theatres specialising in musicals were considered commercial (e.g. Her Majesty's Theatre) as they are the only ones operating without any subsidy. We also made an exception for those large theatres that derived most of their profit from the box office and whose programming showed a heavy commercial slant (e.g. The Melbourne Theatre Company). 'Community' were venues with assured government (or institutional) funding, especially when this resulted in a programming bias: for example Victorian Arts Centre or Melbourne University Student Union Theatre. Most performance spaces, which rely on patchy funding from multiple sources and are staffed by volunteers, were classified as indie.
- in VISUAL ARTS, 'community' galleries have a secure source of funding and are run by artist collectives, a government body, a school or a non-profit organisation. They exhibit mainly the work of their members or members of their community and do not normally engage in selling artworks (e.g. National Gallery of Victoria, Jewish Museum, various university galleries). The difference between 'commercial' and 'indie' galleries is predominantly in the curatorial process and the calibre of artists exhibiting: those galleries that exhibit only by invitation (not accepting proposals) and choose not to represent emerging artists are classified as 'commercial'. We recognise that a number of galleries we classified as 'independent' had long-term commercial aspirations: however, as long as they were prepared to accept proposals and exhibit works by emerging artists and yet retain a curatorial policy which did not consider belonging to a group membership (either professional or demographic) we classified them as 'indie'.
- in CINEMAS, the only 'community' (i.e. fully publicly-funded cinema) is in the Australian Centre for Moving Image and its various incarnations, as all others are profit-making enterprises. 'Commercial' cinemas are owned by chains (Hoyts, Village) and homogeneous in programming, whilst 'independent' cinemas have single owners and a curatorial policy – they may programme short films, arthouse programmes, support Australian film-makers, and engage in other activities unlikely to pay off financially, but cross-subsidised by their normal programming.

Since many venues host different artforms in different ways, the same venue sometimes appears in different categories, sometimes under different names, for example FAD and Eurotrash are, despite the different addresses, one and the same place which operates both as a bar and gallery and occasional performance space. As long as both enterprises were serious efforts, we allowed the entry to double up so that, whilst the dot appears only once on any one map, it may appear on multiple maps specific to the medium.

The information was entered into spreadsheets and sorted to produce a range of maps in Geographic Information System, including separate maps for each medium, for each level of formality, and combinations of all of these, in 1991, 1996, 2001, 2006 and 2009 (Figures 1–5). What follows now are five maps combining indie

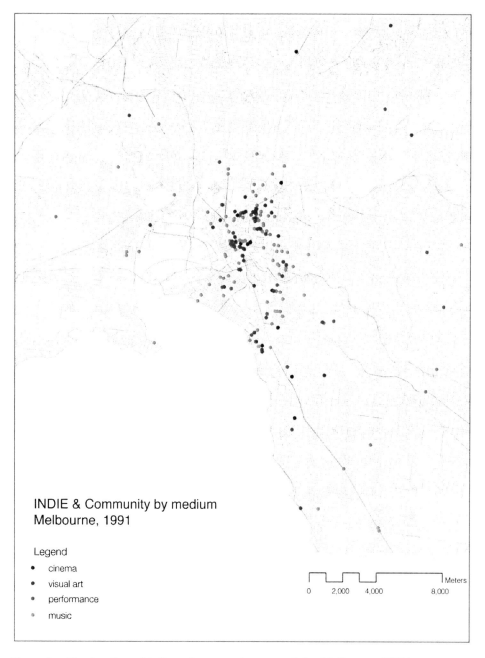

Figure 1. The location of indie and community arts activity, Melbourne (1991).

and community cultural activities involving all four media in inner Melbourne over the 20 years.

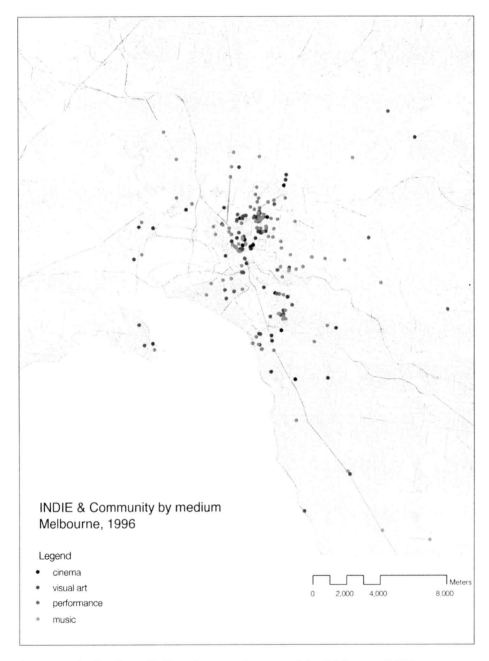

Figure 2. The location of indie and community arts activity, Melbourne (1996).

What's going on?

The maps show a clear emptying out of the arc from the southern suburb of St. Kilda through the south-eastern suburbs of Windsor, Prahran, South Yarra and Richmond. A northward trajectory appears in the last two maps. Most interesting to this particular analysis is the consolidating and intensifying clusters of indie and

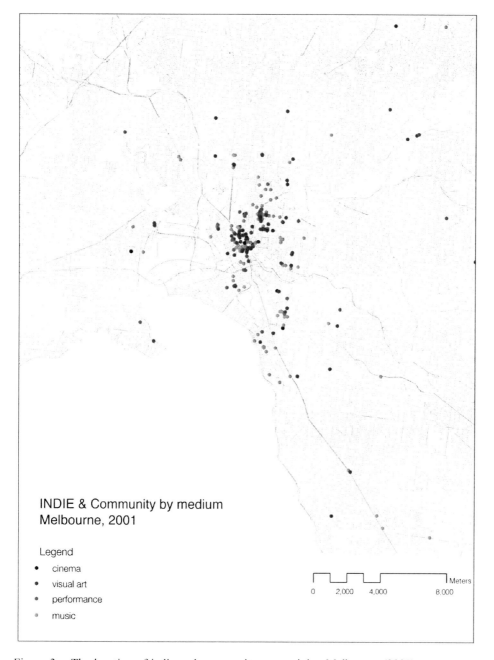

Figure 3. The location of indie and community arts activity, Melbourne (2001).

community cultural activity in the Melbourne city centre and in and around two key streets in the City of Yarra: Gertrude Street, in south-west Fitzroy, and Johnston Street in Collingwood.

The maps were cross-referenced with three further sets of time-series maps showing rates of change of property values (house and apartment prices from the Australian Bureau of Statistics), demographic shifts (income, education and

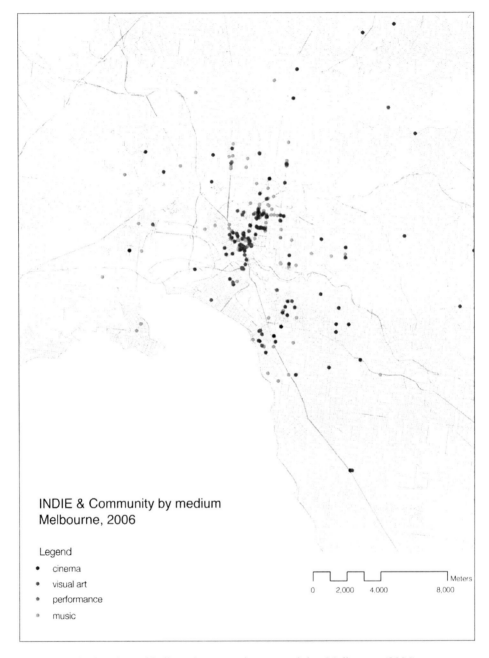

Figure 4. The location of indie and community arts activity, Melbourne (2006).

occupation from census data) and voting patterns in Victorian state elections (1992–2010, from the Victorian Electoral Commission). The combination is a set of maps of gentrification: showing the south-eastern suburbs in inner Melbourne as the most advantaged and rapidly gentrifying, and the suburbs to the north as most disadvantaged and least gentrified. All the inner-city suburbs show significantly higher levels of advantage than the outer suburbs.

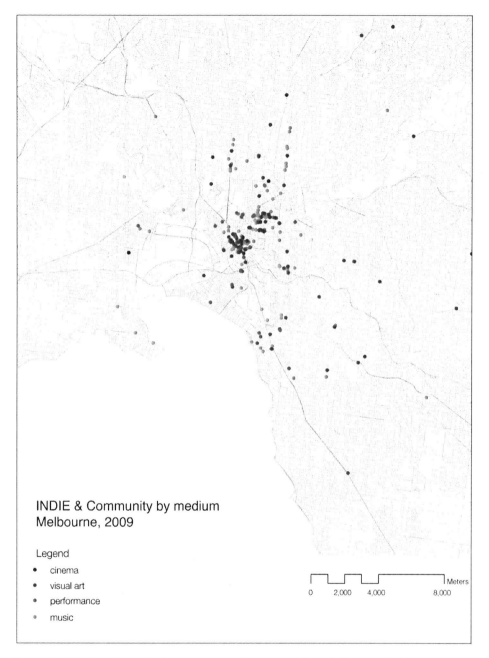

Figure 5. The location of indie and community arts activity, Melbourne (2009).

The expectation for the indie subcultures was that they would move to where the rents are lowest, meaning further north or even off the map to the metropolitan fringe where land is cheapest. But Melbourne is a sprawling city and the outer suburbs lack public transport and infrastructure, significantly reducing their attractiveness. The desire for centrality and easy access for audiences is evidently as important as the rent – the ready potential for interaction with others in the scene was highlighted in interviews with those located in the clusters. It is telling that all three areas with intensive clusters – the city centre, Gertrude Street and Johnston Street – show weak but distinct patterns of a lower rate of increase in property values than in surrounding areas. Residential and commercial rents and sale prices are increasing throughout Melbourne, but according to our analysis of land value data from the Real Estate Institute of Victoria, these three areas contain some of the lowest (and highest) rents in the inner city.

The city centre has a great diversity of building types, sizes, ages, uses and rents, largely due to being the focus of urban development for over 150 years. Heritage and height controls have contributed further to a strong supply of ambient, highly adaptable and easily subdivided spaces, which creates relative affordability for small leasable areas. It is interesting to note that prior to the city council's highly successful campaign in the 1990s to bring residents into the city, the streets were empty at night after the office workers left, but down the laneways and up the fire escapes were the long-time, usually informal homes of artists and musicians and various legal and illegal performance spaces and clubs. These kinds of spaces still proliferate through the city and are still used for cultural activities, although as the number of well-heeled city residents increases, so do the noise complaints. The mainly industrial areas to the north and west of the city centre also have embedded cultural uses, protected in part by industrial and business zonings that prohibit residential use.

For a more complex range of largely social and historical reasons, which are the focus of further papers, Gertrude and Johnston Streets, like the city centre, have remarkable diversity in rents. One of the most striking aspects of both streets and their surrounding areas is the strong concentration of community services such as drug and alcohol programmes, support programmes for indigenous people, and public and community housing and services for their tenants. There appears to be a connection between the cultural activity and community services, with the substantial local appreciation of the less marketable elements of indie subcultures (tolerance of graffiti and loud music) also providing the support necessary for the persistence of community services that may be perceived as carrying greater negative side-effects (such as the local needle exchange). The community services in turn act as something of a brake on gentrification, contributing to the continued presence of the cultural activity.

It is not entirely surprising then that the demographic analysis over time reveals an increase in educational and occupational advantage of residents in the clusters, but a lower rate of increase in economic advantage compared to the rest of the inner city. These residents and business people are Rose's (1984) marginal and early gentrifiers several decades on, well educated but once economically marginal, and still with left-leaning social sensibilities (Ley 1996) that continue to influence the locality. All three areas are safe Australian Labor Party seats, as is the rest of the inner city, with the exception of the north of St. Kilda, Prahran and South Yarra, which are swinging seats and correlate closely with the emptying of the arc.

The implications of these findings for governments wishing to retain or gain creative city status are considerable.

Discussion

The desire for interaction with others in the scene and the need for accessibility for audiences are crucial factors for indie creative subcultures in finding their place. These have to be carefully balanced with their need for cheap rent. The consequence is that the dark pockets of the inner city, with their centrality and relative affordability, are the province of the indie scene. Of course, these dark pockets are also the subject of what Hackworth and Smith (2001) argue is state-sponsored third wave gentrification: under-capitalised sites that with a little planning intervention in the interests of economic development, often with a creative city-inspired inflection, can quadruple in realised value. The dramatic increase in the residential population of the city centre – the successful result of a dedicated government campaign that encourages residential conversion of warehouses and office blocks and also facilitates new-build – not only puts upward pressure on rents but puts new residences right next to existing creative spaces including live music venues.

The retail and industrial areas on the west and northern city edges and in Gertrude and Johnston Streets are the least recapitalised in inner Melbourne. Whilst Gertrude Street is steadily gentrifying without government assistance, the western edge of the city is kept out of the residential land market by its land use zoning, and Johnston Street is still a bit too rough, not quite safe enough – both as a place to consume and as a financial investment – for Florida's (2002) creative class. These latter precincts are the now focus of government concern, and urban renewal strategies are being devised for both.

The city councils responsible for these areas have to make a choice. They can pursue the usual urban renewal/economic development strategy which creates a safer environment for capital investment and increases opportunities for residential development, in which case the indie creative subcultures that both councils celebrate will be displaced far more rapidly and effectively than they anticipate. Or they can grapple with the possibility that maximising the value of land in their municipality not be their primary objective. Inner Melbourne councils are in fact remarkably fortunate by global standards: Australia was relatively well-insulated from the global financial crisis and the inner municipalities have steadily increasing land values and reliably growing rate revenues. Local interest in maintaining the place of creative subcultures in the areas where they currently cluster, and in ensuring there are new areas to allow their continuing evolution, can be supported by a range of planning and policy interventions.

Some of these interventions are already occurring in both municipalities with local and state government cooperation, mainly via the provision of government-managed buildings for low and non-profit creative uses. The more common practice of funding these activities in private buildings continues apace. The siting of such initiatives is crucial: an inspired decision to make the former Collingwood Technical School campus on Johnston Street into a multi-arts complex including a new home for Circus Oz has also created the conditions the Tote Hotel needs to continue as a live music venue (Figure 6). A residential conversion of the old school building, immediately next door to the Tote, would have been disastrous for music at the Tote. As it is, thoughtful intervention seems to have assured the future of both these institutions.

A planning policy that local government can enforce but state government must strengthen is the 'agent of change' principle in the Victorian planning system,

Figure 6. The new home for Circus Oz in Johnston Street, Collingwood, next to the live music venue the Tote Hotel.

which requires the initiator of a new use that might bring about noise complaints (e.g. a new residence next to an existing music venue, or a new music venue next to an existing residence) to provide adequate sound-proofing. The object here is to create a broad urban environment in which multiple uses can co-exist. More effective would be an increase in acceptable music levels in certain locations and contexts, as the live music scene is particularly vulnerable to displacement from increasingly dense and contested inner-urban space.

Most important for councils however is to resist pressures to rezone land to facilitate residential use. As residential use in inner Melbourne is highest and best (economic) land use, and therefore increases the value not just of the land on which it is located but the land around it, and as it is, in addition, the single most incompatible use with independent subcultural activities, there should be areas in the city where it simply does not occur.

Finally, governments at all levels can consider the conditions under which gentrification appears to be limited. Maintenance of community services, provision of social housing where residential use is to be enabled, persistence of industrial uses and fine grain retail areas protected by height and heritage controls all act to varying degrees in different contexts as a brake on gentrification. These conditions, to varying degrees, allow real diversity to shine through – not just cultural diversity but socio-economic diversity, which in various, complex and iterative ways, feed each other.

Conclusion

Melbourne's indie creative subcultures, like similar scenes elsewhere, rely on cheap space and centrality. The ability to co-locate or find spaces big enough to hold multiple uses in order to allow cross-media collaborations, and accommodate the many different roles involved in performance and other activities, is what place-based scenes thrive on. Interaction with others and accessibility to audiences are as important as low rent, and in gentrifying inner cities these can become mutually exclusive. The idea of the creative city as urban renewal strategy creates a paradox: with the success of such strategies measured by decreasing vacancy rates and increasing property values, the primordial soup at the base of all cultural activity dries up. When low and no-profit creative activities are displaced from the city, the evolutionary pool shrinks.

The driving neoliberal imperative for highest and best use of land is anathema to creative subcultures. Governments embarking on urban renewal initiatives have to consider whether their objective is to facilitate maximum capitalisation of land or encourage cultural diversity. Relatively small reforms can be made in the interests of one or the other, with remarkably rapid response in terms of either encouraging gentrification, or creating the conditions for socio-economic diversity – thereby maintaining existing cultural scenes and nurturing new ones. The discussion section of this article details a few such reforms and initiatives. More important is that governments making these decisions appreciate the fundamental contradiction in the concept of the creative city as a means to simultaneously delivering economic development and cultural vitality.

Acknowledgements

The larger research project from which this paper is drawn was an ARC-funded discovery project titled Planning the 'creative city': reconciling global strategies with local subcultures (2009–2011). Thanks to our research assistants Jana Perkovic, Simon Wollan, Elanna Nolan, Megan Harper, Jerome Holleman, Andrew Belegrinos and Ammon Beyerle.

References

Atkinson, R. and Easthope, H., 2009. The consequences of the creative class: the pursuit of creativity strategies in Australia's cities. *International journal of urban and regional research*, 33 (1), 64–79.

Berry, M., 2005. Melbourne – is there life after Florida? *Urban policy and research*, 23 (4), 381–392.

Bianchini, F., 1995. Night cultures, night economies. *Planning practice & research*, 10, 121–126.

Bourdieu, P., 1984[1979]. *Distinction: a social critique of the judgement of taste*. London: Routledge.

Bourdieu, P., 1993. *The field of cultural production*. Cambridge: Polity Press.

Brooks, D., 2000. *Bobos in paradise: the new upper class and how they got there*. New York, NY: Simon & Schuster.

City of Amsterdam, 2003 [online]. Available from: http://www.broedplaatsamsterdam.nl [Accessed March 2003].

De Botton, A., 2004. *Status anxiety*. London: Hamish Hamilton.

Florida, R., 2002. *The rise of the creative class, and how it's transforming work, leisure, community and everyday life*. New York, NY: Basic Books.

Hackworth, J. and Smith, N., 2001. The changing state of gentrification. *Tijdschrift voor Economische en Sociale Geografie*, 94 (4), 464–477.

Hardy, M., 2012. Sunday profile. *Sunday Age*, 2 Sept.

POPULAR MUSIC AND CULTURAL POLICY

Harvey, D., 1993. From space to place and back again: reflections on the condition of post-modernity. *In*: J. Bird, B. Curtis, T. Putnam, G. Robertson, and L. Tickner, eds. *Mapping the futures: local cultures, global change*. London: Routledge, 3–29.

Hebdige, D., 1979. *Subculture: the meaning of style*. London: Methuen.

Hollands, R. and Chatterton, P., 2003. Producing nightlife in the new urban entertainment economy: corporatisation, branding and market segmentation. *International journal for urban and regional research*, 27 (2), 361–385.

Ingleton, S., 2006. *Australian theatre history: the Australian performing group at the Pram Factory* [online]. Available from: http://www.pramfactory.com/family.html.

Kelly, P., 2010 [online]. Available from: http://www.youtube.com/watch?v=ULvW5Xp0IUk [Accessed 13 September 2010].

Kotkin, J., 2005. City of the future. *Washington Post*, 24 July.

Landry, C., 2000. *The creative city: a toolkit for urban innovators*. London: Comedia.

Ley, D., 1996. *The new middle class and the remaking of the central city*. Oxford: Oxford University Press.

Malanga, S., 2004. The curse of the creative class. *Wall Street Journal*, 19 Jan.

Marcus, G., 1989. *Lipstick traces, a secret history of the twentieth century*. London: Martin Secker and Warburg.

McAuliffe, C., 2004. Selling secret lives: subcultures and cultural vitality. *Overland*, 174, 103–105.

McGuigan, J., 2009. Doing a Florida thing: the creative class thesis and cultural policy. *International journal of cultural policy*, 15 (3), 291–300.

Montgomery, J., 2004. Cultural quarters as mechanisms for urban regeneration part 2: a review of four cultural quarters in the UK, Ireland and Australia. *Planning, practice and research*, 19 (1), 3–31.

Peck, J., 2005. Struggling with the creative class. *International journal of urban and regional research*, 29 (4), 740–770.

Porter, L. and Shaw, K., 2009. *Whose urban renaissance? An international comparison of urban regeneration policies*. London: Routledge.

Rose, D., 1984. Rethinking gentrification: beyond the uneven development of Marxist urban theory. *Environment and planning D: society and space*, 1, 47–74.

Shaw, K., 2005. The place of alternative culture and the politics of its protection in Berlin, Amsterdam and Melbourne. *Planning theory and practice*, 6 (2), 151–170.

Shaw, K., 2006. The trouble with the creative class. *Planning news*, 32 (1), 4–5.

Shaw, K., 2009. A curiously qualified legacy of resistance to gentrification. *The Urban Reinventors* [online], (3). Available from: http://www.urbanreinventors.net/paper.php?issue=3&author=shaw.

Smith, N., 2002. New globalism, new urbanism: gentrification as global urban strategy. *Antipode*, 3, 427–450.

Stahl, G., 2004. 'Its like Canada reduced': setting the scene in Montreal. *In*: A. Bennett and K. Kahn-Harris, eds. *After subculture: critical studies in contemporary youth culture*. New York, NY: Palgrave MacMillan, 51–64.

Straw, W., 1991. Systems of articulation, logics of change: communities and scenes in popular music. *Cultural studies*, 5 (3), 368–388.

Throsby, D. and Zednik, A., 2010. *Do you really expect to get paid? An economic study of professional artists in Australia*. Sydney: Australia Council for the Arts.

Timlin, J., 2006. *Pramocracy: the alternative theatre in Carlton, Melbourne, in Sue Ingleton, Australian theatre history: the Australian performing group at the Pram Factory* [online]. Available from: http://www.pramfactory.com/family.html.

Vicario, L. and Martinez Monje, P., 2005. Another 'Guggenheim effect'? Central city projects and gentrification in Bilbao. *In*: R. Atkinson and G. Bridge, eds. *Gentrification in a global context: the new urban colonialism*. London: Routledge, 151–167.

Williams, M., 2006. *The Pram family show, in Sue Ingleton, Australian theatre history: the Australian performing group at the Pram Factory* [online]. Available from: http://www.pramfactory.com/family.html.

Young, I.M., 1990. The ideal of community and the politics of difference. *In*: L. Nicholson, ed. *Feminism/postmodernism*. London: Routledge, 300–323.

'Lend me your ears': social policy and the hearing body

Bruce Johnson

Cultural Studies, Macquarie University, Leura, Australia

Recent developments in music regulation policy in some European countries show a recognition of changes in the built environment, contemporary demographics and the sonic profile of popular music. These initiatives have not been echoed in Australian music policy, where the primary focus is on the cultural and economic conditions of production and consumption, with little interest in the mechanics and biology of sound production and circulation, and their social welfare implications. Within the general category of noise pollution, it appears that the proliferation of low-frequency noise (LFN) is the fastest growing problem, in which contemporary popular music is increasingly implicated. This paper explores why LFN should suddenly become so pervasive that it has begun to attract specific social policy and legislative measures, its own scientific journals, and attempts to establish standards of its measurement specific to a profile that evades traditional sound pollution analysis.

Introduction

This paper grew out of a conference on music policy and regulation, which may be interpreted as a set of measures designed to encourage anything called music. But policy and regulation are also about setting limits to conduct; in this case, constraining what is regarded as the inappropriate deployment of music. The unqualified idealisation of 'music' overlooks the complexities and ambiguities of how sound actually traverses and functions in social formations. Far from constituting an absolute social benefit, music is also a real and measurable source and accompaniment of often lethal social dysfunction. Music policy is therefore about restriction as well as encouragement. On either of those axes, effective policy grows out of the recognition of changes in both music and society, and how the two relate to each other. If that 'map' is not regularly updated in line with such changes, we have a situation analogous to the UN sending aid to a country that no longer exists. Enlightened policy can only emerge from the recognition of changes in the socio-musical map.

In this article, I want to discuss some very particular changes to the contemporary soundscape in the context of longer-term changes in the spaces that host it. Its original focus was music and the urban environment and changes in that relationship since the late twentieth century. In the broader context of this publication, however, I shall also make some reference to analogous changes that have emerged more recently in more rurally based technologies, and which have generated more volatile debates. But it is part of my present argument that the problems in both, albeit very disparate sectors, are much the same in that they both relate to the need to recognise a fundamental change in the contemporary soundscape and the social policy problems that it raises. Those problems are being addressed in a number of continental European countries, even if often in a piecemeal way, and almost invariably without conspicuous recognition of the links between their various sites and discourses: urban and rural, aesthetic and technological. That is, two sets of policy initiatives are emerging from the same fundamental problem, but largely oblivious of each other because each concerns a very different area of social practice. In addition, the musical dimensions of the problem have not officially registered at all as far as I know in Anglo-US music policy, including Australia. The only hint I have encountered of its local recognition is a news item from 2007, in which the Mayor of Sydney, Clover Moore, called for a more nuanced approach to music regulation in urban environments, based on factors other than mere volume, and taking into account pitch and directionality and the different ways in which certain frequencies were circulated and heard (Creagh 2007). In this, she showed a significant insight into the relationship between contemporary music, playback technology, urban living and the human body. And in the debates emerging from the more rurally based technological developments, the sonic aspect of the problem has been all but buried in broader political issues.

Urban space and music

The changes in urban space and demographics of course go back to developments in contemporary urban lifestyles that accelerated during the twentieth century. The first is to do with the nature of contemporary urban space and architecture. Sydney is the model in which I have lived longest, but it is characteristic of urban development since the nineteenth century. The city's superstructures became increasingly modernist from the mid-twentieth century, but constructed upon a pre-modern grid that evolved from the late eighteenth through the nineteenth centuries. The old horizontal and often rather haphazard networks defined by the road system which developed in a pre-modern era and on which the original architecture had been constructed, now had superimposed upon them a completely new vertical order. The visual implications of these changes in urban space have been prolifically elaborated, but not so their acoustic corollaries. From the second half of the twentieth century, high-rise office and apartment blocks replaced old single- to triple-storey terraces, bungalows and retail sites, creating deep and resonant sonic canyons. I illustrate the point with an example I happen to know well. The Vanity Fair Hotel was built around 1900, on the corner of Goulburn and Wentworth Streets in the city (Figure 1). Surrounded by similar structures, it had three above ground storeys and a multi-faceted façade. It was a well-known jazz pub, and I played there from my arrival in Sydney in 1972, until its demolition in 1986.

The building that replaced it is the Sydney headquarters of the Australian Federal Police (Figure 2). Spatially and acoustically, there is not the slightest resemblance between these two buildings, constructed on the same horizontal grid. The transition is representative of twentieth century urban architectural developments. These changes were accompanied by service structures such as supermarkets, shopping malls, cinema complexes, multi-storey car parks, most of them with more sonically reflective and reverberant surfaces and spaces than the structures they

Figure 1. Vanity fair hotel, Sydney.

replaced, and various electrically driven service installations such as lighting and air-conditioning power plants. In addition, high-rise housing and office space stacks its occupants vertically rather than laterally. Sounds made both inside and outside will travel up and down. The relevance of this becomes apparent as we turn to consider sound and the body.

Since the invention of the microphone, musicians have been able to project with greater volume, and music policy has of course recognised this with curfews, acoustic insulation, entertainment licences and location of venues. The rebarbative effects of the sonic environment that has evolved in the era of what I have called the 'Aural Renaissance' (see, e.g. Johnson 2008, p. 58) since the late nineteenth century are, however, far more pervasive than is recognised by public noise pollution legislations. An obvious example is the popularity of the various forms of personal stereo system. In studies of this phenomenon that are oriented towards a Fiskean approach to the reading of popular culture, there has been a strong tendency to romanticise the technology as enabling the emancipative construction of personal sonic space (see, e.g. Bull 2000). From another perspective, however, the personal stereo results in a form of alienation from an environment that demands more attentive engagement, as attested by reports of pedestrian injuries directly attributable to immersion in the acoustic flood coming from earphones. In an increasingly frequent example, police reported that a woman who suffered serious injuries when hit by a van 'was listening to an iPod as she crossed the road' (Kwek 2012). Apart from such accidents, however, sustained use of iPods at high level inevitably results in a degree of irreversible hearing loss that is hardly consistent with creative engagement with the world (see for example Boseley 2010, Bloomfield 2011). Apart from the obvious problem of volume, however, the microphone sounded the beginning of another change in popular music relating to pitch (Johnson 2000, pp. 111–135). That change has been accentuated by subsequent developments in sound technology as well as by culturally based changes in the sonic profile of popular music.

Figure 2. Sydney headquarters of the Australian federal police. Photo: The author.

I emphasise that this development represents a special category of potentially disruptive and traumatic impact, but it is still generally undifferentiated within the larger category of noise pollution. I do not think anyone involved in music policy would dismiss the importance of the regulation of music volume in conurbations. I want to argue the equal importance of another sonic parameter: pitch.

 Here is a striking illustration. In December 2009, a young student attending his first university party in London found himself crowded against a bass speaker. He said to a friend 'My heart feels funny. I think the bass is affecting me. Oh God, I feel very weird. My heart is beating so fast'. Minutes later he collapsed and died. Cause of death was recorded as sudden arrhythmic death syndrome, and, according to a medical spokesperson, possibly attributable to 'a lot of loud noise' (Reid 2009). The slightly bewildered and nebulous diagnosis given by the 'medical spokesman' illustrates how the policy problem I want to discuss has been submerged into the catch-all category of loudness. The clue, however, is in the reference to the bass speaker and sound engineers I spoke to immediately understood what the doctor did not: that the student was probably standing in what is known as a 'bass trap'. But this is just a particularly dramatic and unhappy exemplification of a growing challenge to music policy deliberations: the importance of pitch. There have been some profound changes in the profile of popular music over the last three decades. Apart from the gradual disappearance of silence and, in a number of genres, the contraction of dynamic range, since the advent of the microphone in performance, popular music has begun to deploy lower registers, originally most apparent in female vocalisation (Johnson 2000, pp. 132–135). Since the 1970s that downward movement has also been accelerated through improved bass speakers and manifested as highly amplified and accelerated bass percussion, power chords and drop tuning, the latter of which may lower the pitch of the bottom guitar string by six semitones to a B below its usual E. That is, popular music has become a major contributor to a significant shift in the contemporary soundscape: the increase in low-frequency noise (LFN) or low-frequency sound.[1]

But why should this be of concern to music policy deliberations? LFN exhibits characteristics and produces effects and affects that make it a special category of sound. As a consequence, measurements made under established Environmental Protection Agency (EPA) protocols simply do not record its social impact. Measurement of decibel level does not correspond to nuisance level as registered in complaints and in clinical evaluations. That is, if there is a LFN complaint, it is not enough for the EPA just to measure the volume, because LFN becomes distressing at lower volume than is the case for upper frequencies (Axelsson *et al.* 2007, p. 62, Pawlaczyk-Łuszyńska *et al.* 2007, pp. 319–320). There are physiological as well as psychological reasons for this. The very long wavelengths of LFN, for example, mean that many of the usual masking mechanisms do not work – walls, car windows – which is why we are conscious of the 'doof' effect through walls and ceilings even when we cannot hear the higher registers. One of the masking mechanisms circumvented by LFN is the human head, and to briefly explain the importance of this, it is necessary to use the term 'Ubiquity Effect', elaborated by the acoustic research group CRESSON in Grenoble in France. The Ubiquity Effect refers to the experience of hearing a sound and not being able to identify its source – an aircraft passing overhead, a noise in the house at night, a siren. We are all familiar with the experience, and the emotional effect, which is at the very least a form of anxious curiosity, but which can increase to 'the most uncontrollable panic, including feelings of flight, aggressiveness, or inhibition, perhaps marked with paranoia' (Augoyard and Torgue 2005, p. 137). The Ubiquity Effect produces a feeling of being under threat and powerless in the presence of a superior force. And this is a physiologically grounded response, not only trans-cultural but trans-special (see Johnson 2008). To be exposed episodically to the Ubiquity Effect is undesirable. If large numbers of people are exposed to it as a general condition of life, the outcome is a profoundly dysfunctional community.

So, what kinds of sounds are most likely to produce this rebarbative condition? Remember – it is caused by being exposed to sounds we cannot localise. What kinds of sounds are those? Our primary sound-localisation mechanisms are Inter-Aural Intensity Difference and Inter-Aural Temporal Difference. Both depend on one ear being closer to the source than the other. That ear hears the sound more strongly because the head blocks it from the other, and it also arrives a fraction of a moment before the other ear. And the head then turns and identifies the sound source. Clearly, the optimum conditions for these to work are in the presence of lateral sound and in wavelengths small enough for the head to act as a block. Thus, two kinds of sound are most implicated in producing the trauma of the Ubiquity Effect: sound coming from above (reaching both ears at the same time), or sound having a wavelength longer than the width of the head. The latter is LFN. But, in addition, in the case of LFN, the trauma is not only psychic, but physiological, and indeed, it challenges the mind/body distinction implicit in those two terms. That is because LFN also turns us into a set of resonating chambers and tissues, though not all responding in the same way. The physical and chemical balance of the body becomes disturbed. The result is physical injury that can be potentially fatal.

I want briefly to exemplify some of the trauma associated with LFN. Apart from abundant data available via a Google search (see, e.g. Davies 2012), the following are taken from a collection of articles in the academically peer-reviewed journal (Hansen 2007). Workers and researchers in the field report a range of LFN-specific disorders, including feelings of 'oppression' (Inukai *et al.* 2007, p. 7), 'torment' (Møller and Lydolft 2007, p. 36), 'intrusiveness' and loss of control over their environment (Benton and Abramson-Yehuda 2007, p. 133). A woman whose flat was adjacent to a factory fan exhaust duct experienced psychological disorders of such magnitude as to require professional counselling (Kitamura *et al.* 2007, pp. 191–192). 'LFN places an extra degree of demand upon individuals['] processing and coping strategies' (Benton 2007, p. 237). The 'common theme across studies assessing the subjective impact of LFN has been the tendency for subjects'/ sufferers' annoyance to increase and the quality of lives to degrade over time' (Benton 2007, p. 238). LFN also generates more quantifiable organic damage. Ten subjects experimentally exposed to infrasound for one hour experienced discomfort, pressure in their ears, headaches, fretfulness, fatigue and anxiety. At the same time, all subjects registered disturbances of systolic and diastolic pressure and heart rate, some changes being as high as 30% (Qibai and Shi 2007, p. 309). The potentially fatal condition pneumothorax is triggered by loud low register sounds, in conjunction with other risk factors like alcohol (Johnson and Cloonan 2009, p. 19). Mood-altering organic changes are also suggested in the report that after two hours exposure to LFN at 40 dB(A), 'the normal circadian decline in cortisol concentration was … significantly reduced' (Benton 2007, p. 235). The impact of LFN is not confined to hearing, as in reports that infrasound causes 'visual disturbances … and it has been suggested that some apparently paranormal sightings have been caused by infrasound' (Qistdorff and Poulsen 2007, p. 102). Studies of long-term exposure to noise-induced vibration in workers found an association with 'pericardial thickening, pulmonary fibrosis and so on'. They called the pathological changes 'vibroacoustic disease' (Takahashi *et al.* 2007, p. 250). This is only the briefest sample of LFN-induced disorders (see Johnson 2009).

The broader and growing social impact of LFN is reinforced in a survey of schools conducted by Sweden's Occupational Board of Safety in 1997 which identified a:

> … growing body of data showing that low frequency noise (LFN) differs in its nature from other noises at comparable levels. … Low frequency noise is not only ubiquitous in the general environment but also in the occupational environment (e.g. in industrial control rooms, office-like areas etc.). Ventilation systems, pumps, compressors, diesel engines, gas turbine power stations, means of transport, etc., may be quoted as some

examples of common sources of LFN. Its prevalence in offices and control rooms is mainly due to indoor network installations, ventilation, heating and air-conditioning systems as well as from outdoor sources of noise and poor attenuation of low frequency components by the walls, floors and ceilings. (Pawlaczyk-Łuszyńska *et al.* 2007, pp. 319–320)

This covers pretty much the full spectrum of contemporary urban life. Wherever the LFN problem is being recognised, it is found to be increasing in magnitude: as for example in Japan, Denmark, Sweden and the Netherlands. Regarding his own region, Rotterdam, an EPA inspector writing around 2003, made the following projection:

In 15 years 1/3 (1/2 in all Holland) of the Rotterdam inhabitants will be over 55 years of age. At the moment most of the LFS-complainants are in this age group. The shared use of buildings for 'industrial' and 'living' purposes is increasing … At the moment only 3% of Dutch homes are provided with climate control installations. These are sources of LFS and the numbers will grow. Due to the lack of building space more underground infrastructure is being developed. Vibrations caused by traffic result in LFS via the foundations of residential buildings. (Sloven 2007a, p. 82)

That is, a sonic profile which generates a range of traumas from anxiety to panic is an increasingly pervasive aspect of 'normal' life.

For the reasons I have sketched above, music is now one of the main sources of this trauma. Amplified music is not only mentioned frequently in summaries of complaint patterns; it has climbed close to the top of the list. In a 1985 study, it was outranked in nuisance value by most other categories of LFN. In a 1989 study, amplified music or 'discotheque' ranked second and amongst documented studies have remained in that position, behind the sound of a drop forge, both causing particular nuisance because they are impulse LFN (Qistdorff and Poulsen, 2007, p. 89, Poulsen 2007a, p. 141, 2007b, pp. 181, 187). We do not hear many drop forges, but we are constantly immersed in music, whether or not of our own choosing. All the evidence suggests that LFN is a growing problem overall, and that within that framework, amplified music is its fastest growing problem. A professional environmental noise officer in the Netherlands reports the need to use what is called a 'C-weighting' noise nuisance measurement system that specifically targets LFN:

Due to the problems arising from musical festivals in the Netherlands and in Belgium the C-weighting has become of huge importance. … More and more of the organisers are becoming aware that the lower frequencies are very important in terms of disturbance. The implementation of C-weighted monitoring and the use of C-weighted level defined licences are a part of the solution. In some cases all noise in the octaves of 32 Hz and lower is forbidden, the participants do not hear the difference but they just miss some of the sensation in their stomachs …

At longer distances the control of noise levels shows that reductions in low frequency content at source have an important role in reducing annoyance. Local authorities are becoming more aware of these factors and are conscious of the importance of the weighting problem in measurements. LFN is being recognised as a significant issue. (Sloven 2007b, pp. 222–223)

The problem is of particular magnitude in contemporary space because there is a profound dissonance between those sonic developments, high-rise modernist architecture and the physiology of hearing.

In the context of this paper, it is relevant that increasing numbers of European governments are factoring LFN into their music regulation policies. The rising LFN content, along with Sound Pressure Level (perceived volume), in popular music is being recognised in quantification standards and regulatory and licensing procedures. In Nijmegen, a specific measuring and licensing standard is also applied to music events in which LFN is audible: a 'penalty' of 5 dB(A) is added to compliance protocols (Sloven 2007b, p. 224). Over the last decade or so, it is increasingly understood that LFN requires specialised attention, as witnessed by the inauguration of the scientific journal *LFN* from which many of the sources cited here are drawn. In Denmark, sufferers from exposure formed an active lobby group called Infralydens Fjender (Enemies of Infrasound) (Møller and Lydolft 2007, p. 30). Denmark was amongst the first to implement state interventions. In 1997, the Danish EPA recommended that the regulation of the volume of indoor noise should be lower than for higher frequencies. Denmark also recognises the higher nuisance potential of 'impulse' over continuous noise, adding a 5 dB penalty for the former (Poulsen 2007b, p. 187). 'Low frequency impulse noise' is a good description of much if not most contemporary pop, particularly hip hop and metal, as manifested in the notorious 'doof, doof' effect mentioned above that is heard from neighbouring apartments, car sound systems and from venues where such genres are played. In 1996, Sweden introduced specific guidelines for the regulation and measurement of LFN, also recognising that its nuisance potential required 'penalty' provisions relating to volume and intermittency. Germany, Poland and the Netherlands have also developed LFN-specific protocols (Imaizumi *et al.* 2007, p. 158, Poulsen 2007a, pp. 142–152, Subedi *et al.* 2007, p. 200).

Wind turbines and LFN

None of what I have described has registered in official Australian music policy. The closest we have come to a public debate on the growing problems of LFN has arisen in the course of controversies over wind turbines. The transition from music to industrial technology might at first seem incongruous, but I wish to emphasise that what they share here is the same profile of sonic toxicity. In my concluding comments I shall suggest that it is the apparent incongruity which is in itself a major reason that the problem is still addressed so inadequately, and why they should therefore be linked. These debates have become increasingly polarising, volatile and so broadly politicised as to encompass arguments on issues including climate change, renewable energy, economics, visual aesthetics, the qualifications of participants and the veracity of those who feel they are economic and/or health victims of nearby wind farms. They have produced strange bedfellows, drawing together climate change deniers with environmental groups in alliances in which the question of the need for alternative energy sources becomes conflated with the question of their effectiveness. Thus, someone who calls for further research into the possible dangers to health of those who live in proximity to wind turbines is likely to be characterised as a climate change denier by those with an investment in wind farms. The dissonant convergence was recently exemplified in connection with an article on wind farms in the online journal *New Matilda*, which drew an unprecedented number and bewildering range of often virulent responses involving alliances that shifted as they were posted (Keane 2012). It is ironic and dispiriting that an industrial sector apparently committed to developing environmentally sustainable energy sources, and who therefore also have a vested economic interest in wind farm development, has fallen back upon similar smear tactics to those which were employed by tobacco companies against the anti-smoking health lobby.

My observations regarding the policy implications arising from LFN and wind turbines are thus presented in a rather intimidating discursive context and with appropriate caution and restraint. It is repeatedly declared by advocates of wind farms that there is no peer-reviewed evidence that wind farms represent a danger to health. Not even the qualification 'no peer reviewed evidence' was included in the position taken by Mr Ken Andrew McAlpine, Director, Policy and Government Relations, Asia-Pacific Region, of the Danish-based Vestas Australian Wind Technology Pty Ltd, at an enquiry by the Commonwealth of Australia Senate enquiry into the social and economic impact of rural wind farms in March 2011 (Commonwealth of Australia 2011). McAlpine declared unequivocally that 'There is nothing about wind turbines that is unsafe. There is nothing about them that is unhealthy' (Commonwealth of Australia 2011, p. CA1). 'In Denmark in particular, in Germany and in many of the other countries in Europe where thousands of wind turbines have been installed, old ones and modern ones, there are not any health claims' (Commonwealth of Australia 2011, p. CA2). It is important again to emphasise therefore that almost all the data presented above regarding the dangers of LFN are from a collection of articles from a journal that I have taken care to ensure is academically reviewed at the most rigorous level, including a personal assurance from the editor, Emeritus Professor Colin H. Hansen (2012). Mr McAlpine's testimony to the Senate hearing, referred to above, that 'there are not any health claims' is absolute and unequivocal, from someone who may be expected to be listening for them. One of the articles in Hansen's collection of essays (Møller and Lydolft 2007), however, reports the results of a survey of 198 complaints about LFN and infrasound, conducted by the Department of acoustics, at Denmark's Aalborg University. These report that for 'nearly all' respondents, LFN constitutes a 'torment' (Møller and Lydolft 2007, p. 105) that impairs quality of life, and I referred above to the public lobby group in Denmark called Enemies of Infrasound. One might reasonably expect McAlpine, representing a Danish-based company, to be aware of this, especially since the president of the society, Solveig Odderskov corresponded with the Danish Prime Minister, amongst many other public officials and instrumentalities, on the subject (see Anon 2012a, Odderskov 2012). I mention Denmark because it is the home base of Mr McAlpine's company, and he specifically included Denmark in his disclaimer. Farther afield one can access 105 other sites recording protests, amongst which health concerns provide the most prominent basis, regarding wind turbines from all over the globe (Anon 2012b). This is not necessarily to validate them, but to note that the claim that there are 'no health complaints' is inconsistent with a considerable and easily accessible body of data.

One of the primary factors in these concerns is LFN. Dr John Etherington is Reader in Ecology at the University of Wales, former co-editor of the Journal of Ecology, and Thomas Huxley Medallist at the Royal College of Science. In the context of the debates over wind farms, it seems important to cite such honorifics. The title of his book, *The Wind Farm Scam*, certainly advertises a general position, but the material I wish to cite concentrates on only one aspect of his study, that is, noise, and what he has to say on the subject is confirmed by the other academic work I have cited. The two main sources of noise emanating from a wind turbine are the LFN of the turbine blades themselves, the gearbox and generator. Apart from the noise of the wake vortices, as the blades pass the tower there is 'a pulsating quality' added to the sound pattern. In addition, where there are clusters of turbines, as they pass in and out of phase with each other, there are 'beat' sounds set-up (Etherington 2009, p. 113), so that apart from LFN itself, there is a further nuisance factor, known as aerodynamic modulation; the profile is not unlike that of the impulse patterns associated with forms of pop music rich in LFN. Indeed, it is a sound which Etherington in passing, but instructively in this context, likens to the woofer in a music sound system (Etherington 2009, p. 114; see similarly p. 115). He reports that complaints about this noise extended up to 1.9 km away from the turbine, notwithstanding developer's claims that the limit is 0.5 m. As in so many of the studies in Hansen, he cites cases in which owners of properties in proximity to turbines have suffered health problems, even to the extent of having to abandon their homes (Etherington 2009, pp. 118–119). It is difficult to disentangle the respective impacts of LFN and aerodynamic modulation in this problem, just as it is impossible to predict the problems by means of the usual decibel (Db) projections made by technicians working with the wind farm developers. As documented above, the nuisance level of LFN cannot be estimated through traditional Db measurement in the most stable situations; far less when complicated by variables such as air temperature, topography, wind direction and varieties of domestic architecture. But when occupiers, especially those who initially welcomed the rental income from a wind farm, begin to report radical deterioration of the standard of life and even abandon their homes, some credence should be given to the complaints, or at the very least further research be undertaken. That there is some kind of problem with wind farms near human habitation – economic or health-related – seems to be recognised in Denmark; air passengers arriving in Copenhagen will be familiar with a score of so of wind turbines constructed in the sea just off the coast. But if LFN is so disturbing and disorienting when transmitted through air, how much damage might it inflict on sonar directed marine life via the greater conductivity of water (see, for example, Vella 2012)?

Conclusions

The concern of this article, however, is with cultural policy, not environmental issues. Yet, by way of conclusion, that is part of the problem. That is, our way of taxonomising social discourses is one of the reasons that the phenomenon of LFN has remained only intermittently audible. There is little crossover between the literature of popular music and of environmental ecology, so that the pervasiveness of LFN as a potentially traumatic condition of contemporary life is occluded. Apart from brief figurative collisions such as the examples above, environmentalists do not read or write in the field of music and vice versa. Yet even within each of these fields, LFN has been about to hide in the interstices, or to camouflage itself as something else, just as a headache caused by a tumour can be diagnosed as a sinus problem. Because the wind farm debate ranges over so many issues, the specific role of LFN as a more general problem of contemporary life has been all but submerged under partisan political arguments over other issues. Likewise, in discussion of music, LFN as a distinctive and potentially traumatic element in its sonic profile has been eclipsed by debates about volume, anti-social lyrics or festival riots. And in larger policy discussions about noise pollution, LFN is overwhelmed by questions of volume. Each of these areas of social policy has its own discourse, its own lobby groups and government instrumentalities. The ways of dividing up policy responsibilities discourage those who monitor urban acoustic issues such as entertainment licences, from interesting themselves in, for example, alternative energy sources. If we were able to redraw the map of the forces that traverse our society and our social welfare, new lines of force would appear, new policy continuities. If the increasingly pervasive phenomenon of LFN was to be extrapolated as a distinctive issue, then attention could be shifted to the policy problems presented by an acoustic phenomenon that affects the totality of the contemporary soundscape, a connection could be recognised between the death of a freshman university student at a party in London and the depression and organic damage suffered by someone living near a wind farm in rural Australia, or a pathological aberration in the life cycle of a marine species.

I began with what is at this time the more ubiquitous impact of popular music. The LFN phenomenon suggests conclusions that raise significant issues of social policy in the contemporary contexts of urban space and the sonic character and portability of popular music. LFN is a growing problem, in which music is prominently implicated, but it is only one of a disparate array of problems requiring that existing noise regulations need to be revised to become LFN specific. The role of trans-cultural and infra-cultural features of auditory physiology is central to the sonic definition of power relations. Official music policy in Australia has failed to take into account the changing dynamics in the relationship between the sonic profile of pop music and the circulation of sound in urban spaces. To fulfil its social responsibilities, it must extend its interests to a more fully informed understanding of the mechanics of sounding and the physiology of hearing. Without the kinds of policy interventions taking place in increasing numbers of countries in Continental Europe, it seems that certain spatial contexts for music and certain characteristics of music itself are inherently incapable of generating humane sonic environments.

Acknowledgements

This paper draws together and extends strands from various publications that have been generated by over a decade of research in the field, as well as previous conference/ symposium presentations, including at the Institute of Popular Music, Liverpool UK in 2007, for the World Forum for Acoustic Ecology at Koli in Finland, June 2010, and the 'Policy Notes: Popular Music, Industry and the State' conference in Melbourne, June 2012. I wish to express my thanks to colleagues at those events and in other discussions who have helped me to refine the thoughts underpinning this paper. The topic on this occasion, which focuses on music policy in Australia, generates some new material, with a new assemblage and emphasis.

Note

1. Some useful figures for perspective: The average range of human hearing is generally taken to from 20 to 20,000 Hz. The lowest sound on the piano keyboard is 27.5 Hz, the highest is 4186. The usual range of the human voice is between 400 and 3000 Hz. LFN is usually defined as the range 20–200 Hz. Infrasound is taken to be below 20 Hz.

References

Anon, 2012a. *Danes, turbines, and 'infralydens fjender' ('enemies of infrasound')* [online]. Available from: http://www.windturbinesyndrome.com/2012/danes-wind-turbines-and-infralydens-fjender-enemies-of-infrasound/ [Accessed 8 October 2012].

Anon, 2012b. *Civil disobedience & other protest* [online]. Available from: http://www.wind-turbinesyndrome.com/category/civil-disobedience-other-protest/?var=wts [Accessed 9 October 2012].

Augoyard, J.-F., and Torgue, H., eds. 2005. *Sonic experience: a guide to everyday sounds*, trans. Andra McCartney and David Paquette. Montreal: McGill-Queen's University Press.

Axelsson, P., Holmberg, K., and Landström, U., 2007. Low frequency noise and annoyance in the classroom. *In*: C.H. Hansen, ed. *The effects of low-frequency noise and vibration on people*. Brentwood Essex: Multi-Science Publishing, 61–70.

Benton, S., 2007. Low frequency noise annoyance and the negotiation challenge for environmental officers and sufferers. *In*: C.H. Hansen, ed. *The effects of low-frequency noise and vibration on people*. Brentwood Essex: Multi-Science Publishing, 227–244.

Benton, S., and Abramson-Yehuda, O., 2007. Low frequency noise annoyance: the behavioural challenge. *In*: C.H. Hansen, ed. *The effects of low-frequency noise and vibration on people*. Brentwood Essex: Multi-Science Publishing, 131–136.

Bloomfield, C., 2011. Turn down the volume! Loud iPods overtake noisy workplaces as most common cause of hearing damage. *Daily Mail online*, 23 December 2011 [online]. Available from: http://www.dailymail.co.uk/health/article-2078048/Loud-iPods-common-cause-hearing-damage-irritate-fellow-passengers.html#ixzz28Cf1t7ct [Accessed 9 October 2012].

Boseley, S., 2010. Young iPod users risk permanent hearing damage, warns expert; Many MP3 players produce noise intensity of an aircraft taking off, says Yale's associate professor of medicine. *The Guardian online*, Wednesday 21 April [online]. Available from: http://www.guardian.co.uk/technology/2010/apr/21/young-ipod-users-risk-hearing-damage [Accessed 9 October 2012].

Bull, M., 2000. *Sounding out the city: personal stereos and the management of everyday life*. Oxford, NY: Berg.

Commonwealth of Australia, 2011. Proof committee hansard, senate community affairs references committee, reference: social and economic impact of rural wind farms [online], 29 March, Melbourne. This is a PDF in my possession of an uncorrected Hansard proof; the final report is available at: http://aefweb.info/data/Senate%20Report%20on%20Wind%20Farms%20230611.pdf

Creagh, S., 2007. Mayor blasts super speakers that give out bad vibes. *Sydney Morning Herald*, 24 July [online]. Available from: http://www.smh.com.au/news/national/super-speakers-give-out-bad-vibes/2007/07/23/1185043033305.html [Accessed 24 July 2007].

Davies, A., 2012. *Acoustic trauma: bioeffects of sound* [online]. Available from: http://schizophonia.com/installation/trauma/trauma_thesis/index.htm [Accessed 8 October 2012].

Etherington, J., 2009. *The wind farm scam: an ecologist's evaluation*. London: Stacey International.

Hansen, C.H., 2007. *The effects of low-frequency noise and vibration on people*. Brentwood Essex: Multi-Science Publishing. This is a collection of reprints from the *Journal of Low Frequency Noise*, covering the period 2000–2005 inclusive – see Introduction, vii – though the individual papers are not dated or sourced.

Hansen, C.H., 2012. Re review process of the journal low frequency noise. 2 October. Personal communication to author at brujoh@utu.fi.

Imaizumi, H., Takahashi, Y., Jinguuji, M., and Kunimatsu, S., 2007. Blast densification method: sound propagation and estimation of psychological and physical effects. *In*: C.H. Hansen, ed. *The effects of low-frequency noise and vibration on people*. Brentwood Essex: Multi-Science Publishing, 157–176.

Inukai, Y., Nakamura, N., and Taya, H., 2007. Unpleasantness and acceptable limits of low frequency sound. *In*: C.H. Hansen, ed. *The effects of low-frequency noise and vibration on people*. Brentwood: Multi-Science, 7–13.

Johnson, B., 2000. *The inaudible music: jazz, gender and Australian modernity*. Sydney: Currency Press.

Johnson, B., 2008. 'Quick and dirty': sonic mediations and affect. *In*: C. Birdsall and A. Enns, eds. *Sonic mediations: body, sound, technology*. Cambridge: Cambridge Scholars, 43–60.

Johnson, B., 2009. Low frequency noise and urban space. *Popular Music History*, 4 (2), 177–195.

Johnson, B. and Cloonan, M., 2009. *Dark side of the tune: popular music and violence.* Farnham: Ashgate.

Keane, S., 2012. Future shock: Waubra fights the anti-wind bullies. *New Matilda*, 26 September [online]. Available from: http://newmatilda.com/2012/09/26/antiwind-problem-waubra [Accessed 26 September 2012].

Kitamura, T., Hasebe, M., and Yamada, S., 2007. Psychological analysis of complaints on noise/low frequency noise and the relation between psychological response and brain structure. *In*: C.H. Hansen, ed. *The effects of low-frequency noise and vibration on people*. Brentwood Essex: Multi-Science Publishing, 191–198.

Kwek, G., 2012. Sydney teen badly hurt after being struck by van while listening to iPod. *Sydney Morning Herald*, 22 May [online]. Available from: http://www.smh.com.au/nsw/sydney-teen-badly-hurt-after-being-struck-by-van-while—listening-to-ipod-20120522-1z1vr.html [Accessed 9 October 2012].

Møller, H. and Lydolft, M., 2007. A questionnaire survey of complaints of infrasound and low-frequency noise. *In*: C.H. Hansen, 2007, pp. *The effects of low-frequency noise and vibration on people*. Brentwood Essex: Multi-Science Publishing, 105-118. Available from: http://vbn.aau.dk/files/54564032/Moller_and_Lydolf_2002.pdf [Accessed 8 October 2012].

Odderskov, S., 2012. *Landsforeningen Infralydens Fjender* [online]. Available from: http://www.windturbinesyndrome.com/wp-content/uploads/2012/04/fogh03feb02.pdf [Accessed 8 October 2012].

Pawlaczyk-Łuszyńska, M., with Dudariwicz, A., Waszkowska, M., Szymczak, W., Kameduła, M., Śliwinska-Kowalska, M., 2007. Does low frequency noise at moderate levels influence human performance? *In*: C.H. Hansen, ed. *The effects of low-frequency noise and vibration on people*. Brentwood Essex: Multi-Science Publishing, 319–341.

Poulsen, T., 2007a. Comparison of objective methods for assessment of annoyance of low frequency noise with the results of a laboratory listening test. *In*: C.H. Hansen, ed. *The effects of low-frequency noise and vibration on people*. Brentwood Essex: Multi-Science Publishing, 137–156.

Poulsen, T., 2007b. Annoyance of low frequency noise (LFN) in the laboratory assessed by LFN-sufferers and non-sufferers. *In*: C.H. Hansen, ed. *The effects of low-frequency noise and vibration on people*. Brentwood Essex: Multi-Science Publishing, 177–190.

Qibai, C.Y.H. and, Shi, H. 2007. An investigation of the physiological and psychological effects of infrasound on persons. *In*: C.H. Hansen, ed. *The effects of low-frequency noise and vibration on people*. Brentwood Essex: Multi-Science Publishing, 303–310.

Qistdorff, F. R. and Poulsen, T., 2007. Annoyance of low frequency noise and traffic noise. *In*: C.H. Hansen, ed. *The effects of low-frequency noise and vibration on people*. Brentwood Essex: Multi-Science Publishing, 87–91.

Reid, T., 2009. Loud bass music 'killed student'. *Metro*, 9 December [online]. Available from: http://www.metro.co.uk/news/805430-loud-bass-music-killed-student-tom-reid [Accessed 9 December 2009].

Sloven, P., 2007a. A Structured approach to LFS-complaints in the Rotterdam region of the Netherlands. *In*: C.H. Hansen, ed. *The effects of low-frequency noise and vibration on people*. Brentwood Essex: Multi-Science Publishing, 71–85.

Sloven, P., 2007b. LFN and the A-weighting. *In*: C.H. Hansen, ed. *The effects of low-frequency noise and vibration on people*. Brentwood Essex: Multi-Science Publishing, 219–226.

Subedi, J.K., Yamaguchi, H., Matsumoto, Y., and Ishara, M., 2007. Annoyance of low frequency tones and objective evaluation methods. *In*: C.H. Hansen, ed. *The effects of low-frequency noise and vibration on people*. Brentwood Essex: Multi-Science Publishing, 199–218.

Takahashi, Y., Kanada, K., and Yonekawa, Y. 2007. Some characteristics of human body surface vibration induced by low frequency noise. *In*: C.H. Hansen, ed. *The effects of low-frequency noise and vibration on people*. Brentwood Essex: Multi-Science Publishing, 249–264.

Vella, G., 2012. *The Environmental Implications of Offshore Wind Generation* [online]. Available from: http://vella.UtilitiesProject.com [Accessed 9 October 2012].

Why get involved? Finding reasons for municipal interventions in the Canadian music industry

Richard Sutherland

Department of Policy Studies, Mount Royal University, Calgary, Alberta, Canada

This article investigates the role of Canadian municipal governments in relation to the development of music industry policy. It examines two attempts by Canadian cities (Calgary and Toronto) to develop municipally based music policies. Both cases are examined in context of the policies of other levels of government in Canada, where municipalities have not generally played a significant role in addressing the music industry. Historically, music industry policy has been a concern of federal government policies. The article addresses how this creates a particular conception of the industry and the extent to which municipal policies need to challenge this in order to be effective. Further, the article examines some of the other factors that constrain and shape the ability of Canadian municipalities to intervene in this field.

Canada: a leader in music industry policy?

This paper deals with attempts in Canadian cities to develop local music industry policies. One in the Western Canadian city of Calgary initiated by the city's arts development agency late in 2007 has, so far, failed to achieve much. Another much more detailed proposal, emerging from the Toronto-based recording industry, was announced in June of 2012 but to this point has remained merely that – a proposal, at least at the municipal level. In doing so, the paper examines the various reasons why the former initiative went nowhere and the latter initiative may remain unrealized. Some of these may seem relatively obvious, such as lack of adequate funding but this lack is itself merely indicative of other issues that contributed to the Calgary initiative's failure. The paper also asks why Calgary's cultural policy-makers attempted to develop such a policy. These reasons are not so obvious, not even, perhaps, to the policy-makers.

Following O'Brien's and Miles's (2010) emphasis on local conditions as critical to any analysis of local cultural policy, one can and should look to Calgary's unique set of circumstances in order to understand both the attempt and the failure. There are, however, limits to this approach. Whilst Calgary's circumstances may be unique, the intended object of policy (in this case the music industry) is understood as much more than a local or even national phenomenon. Those aspects of the music industry present in Calgary are not in themselves especially distinctive. Nor is the policy apparatus available to Calgary's local government entirely unique. Canadian municipalities have a relatively similar set of powers and responsibilities that result from their place within Canada's political system. The significance of Calgary's local conditions for the attempted development of a music industry policy cannot be fully understood without some of this more general context. Thus, the paper is also an exploration of the wider issue of Canadian municipalities and their capacity to develop meaningful policy for the music industry and it is here that we will begin.

Canada has often been viewed as a leader in music industry policy; many Canadian policies in this field, such as the Canadian content broadcast quotas for commercial radio or the Sound Recording Development Program and its successor, the Canada Music Fund, are held up as models for similar measures in other countries (Malm and Wallis 1992, Shuker 1994). These are also amongst the most widely admired and durable cultural policies within Canada, surviving (and even expanding) for 40 and 25 years, respectively (Straw 1993). Yet, when it comes to the involvement of local government in developing music industries, Canada lags far behind other countries, most notably Britain and Australia, but also the United States. In contrast to these countries where the music industry has been the object of local policies, there are only the vague beginnings of this amongst Canadian cities.

One explanation for the lack of municipal music industry policies in Canada may very well be the prominence of its federal policies, which may inhibit both local governments and music industry interest groups from viewing the music industry as a matter of local concern. In Britain, where for many years the national government remained relatively uninvolved, a number of local governments were actively engaged in the support and promotion of music industry activity (Frith 1993). This support has taken a number of forms, from Norwich council's support of a local venue for popular music (Street 1993) to Sheffield's 'Music Factory' programme (Frith 1993, p. 15–16). Policies aimed at developing the music industry in the United States, where they exist at all, are carried out primarily by local governments. Austin's ongoing strategy of fostering local music industry activity through promotion and cultivation of a welcoming environment for owners of clubs and bars is well documented (Shank 1994, Titan Music Group 2012). Miami's strategy for attracting music businesses through tax breaks (described in Miller and Yudice 2002) made it a centre for the international Latin music business. Australia furnishes further examples of municipal involvement in music industry policy (Gibson and Homan 2004, Homan 2008). Melbourne in particular provides perhaps the most comprehensive music industry policy from a local government, with an integrated approach that encompasses support for businesses, promotion, advocacy, education and training, as well as sensitivity to zoning and licensing issues (City of Melbourne 2010). Such examples are illustrative of the possibilities for music industry policies carried out at a local level but they also stand in contrast to some of the emphases we find in Canada's nationally conceived approach to the music industry.

Each level of government has particular strengths in policy-making but the predominance of one level will tend to position the music industry as an object of policy in a particular way (Paquette 2008, p. 304, Lascoumes and Le Galès 2012, p. 72–74). That is, the policies and approaches that governments use are to some extent constitutive of their objects. Another way of seeing this is the ways in which policies are framed, which enact particular versions of objects whilst suppressing possible versions (Schön and Rein 1995, p. 23–26). If the music industry in Canada is to some extent defined by the suite of policies the federal government has directed towards it, then it is a matter of national identity, a source of programming for radio broadcasters and, most important, primarily a sound recording industry. Again, some of these characteristics effectively position the music industry in Canada, whose concerns are outside the responsibility or jurisdiction of local governments. This is most clear in terms of the music industry's role as a supplier of programming for broadcasting, which in Canada is exclusively under federal jurisdiction; this effectively precludes any significant involvement from any other level of government.

National

The national scope of music industry policy has implications for its effects at a local level. These policies have their greatest impact in existing centres such as Toronto (still the location of most of Canada's recording industry) and Montreal, as well as, to a much lesser extent, Vancouver. This makes these policies less relevant for Calgary's still nascent music industry. Indeed, the city, along with the rest of the province of Alberta, secures much less funding from federal programmes than its share of the population would suggest (Sutherland 2013). Federal cultural policy in Canada has also generally concerned itself with questions of national sovereignty and unity but these concerns are by their nature not always adequately attuned to local conditions and expressions of culture. Nationalism has been an awkward fit with popular music analysis in English Canada (Shepherd 1993, p. 179–181). Particular scenes and locales have arguably been more important sites for the linkage of music and territory, not only in Canada but elsewhere. Liverpool, San Francisco, Austin and more recently cities such as Seattle and Williamsburg have served to designate certain moments or movements within the history of popular music. Closer to home, Montreal is an example of a Canadian city becoming widely known and acclaimed over the past decade as a particularly fertile locale for popular music, led by artists such as Arcade Fire, Godspeed You! Black Emperor and Grimes.

Sound recording as the music industry

The identification of sound recording with the music industry presents a different sort of implication. There is a large amount of music industry activity that is not adequately addressed by the suite of policies delivered by federal government. Most of those involved in creating popular music will never reach the level where the sound recording industry-oriented federal programmes are of any relevance to them. The roughly $10 million in grants annually from the federal government is targeted mostly at record labels. Provincial programmes directed at the music industry are likewise focused for the most part on sound recording. Canadian content is, of course, only relevant for those record labels and recording artists that receive airplay on broadcast radio or for the composers of the songs they record. The broadcast policies aimed at developing talent tend to direct their resources at federally oriented organisations such as FACTOR.[1] This is an issue that caused some dissension at the last policy hearings on radio held by Canada's regulatory body the Canadian Radio-Television and Telecommunications Commission (CRTC) in 2006. The majority of copyright policy (the other major strand of Canadian music industry policy) does little or nothing to support aspects of the music industry outside sound recording and music publishing.[2]

It is not the merits of these policies that are at issue here but their narrow scope. Sound recording is only one of several music industries, including live performance, music publishing, instrument manufacturing and others. The continued centrality of recording to the music industries is questionable, given that the value of the sector has been on a fairly steady decline over the past decade. A 2012 study funded by Music Canada (the association represents primarily the Canadian divisions of major labels) put the value of the Canadian recording industry in 2011 at C$414 million, a decline of 22% from four years previously (Music Canada 2012, p. 2). The same report assessed the economic impacts of both the recording industry and of live music performances in Canada, with the former estimated at C$530.8 million in 2009 and the latter valued at $455.2 million in 2010 (Music Canada 2012, p. 4). The relative value of the industries makes the near exclusive focus of government policies on recording somewhat difficult to justify on economic grounds alone.

Nonetheless, it is clear that music industry policy has been framed in these terms and there have only been tentative steps to embrace a wider array of music industries. To some extent, recording industry representatives may have successfully positioned themselves to speak to governments on behalf of music industries generally (Williamson and Cloonan 2007, p. 306–309). But government policies have reinforced this situation through the statistics they collect, the names for their programmes and, above all, the measures these programmes contain. The result is that when policy-makers speak of 'the music industry' in effect they usually mean the recording industry. If, as Lascoumes and Le Galès suggest, such policies define their object, then any municipality contemplating such a strategy would be likely to see the music industry in these terms, privileging policies that pertain to sound recording and ignoring policies that might be more oriented towards other music industries, particularly live performance.

What can Canadian cities do and why?

The above policy frames may structure the way in which Canadian cities view their potential involvement with the music industry. But there are other factors specific to local governments themselves that also enable and limit their ability to intervene in this field of policy. Municipalities are the least empowered of the three levels of government in Canada's federal system. Municipalities are a provincial jurisdiction and to some degree exist at the pleasure of the provincial governments, on a similar footing to universities or school boards. They have fairly limited powers of legislation (confined to by-laws) and few sources of revenue, relying for the most part on property taxes, business taxes and user fees and fines alongside provincial grants for certain capital projects. Because they are under provincial jurisdiction, any federal grants to cities must be directed through provincial governments, which may or may not pass on these amounts in full. And whilst municipal governments can borrow money for capital projects, they cannot run an operating deficit, which further limits their spending power (Federation of Canadian Municipalities 2012, p. 4–9). All of this means that cities are far less able to fund programmes than the provinces, let alone the federal government.

There are a number of reasons why Canadian municipal governments might decide to support a local music industry, similar to those that obtain in other jurisdictions. Some of the more effective rationales for locally oriented music industry policy elsewhere have been derived from the need to create youth employment, to stimulate economic development or to encourage social engagement (Frith 1993, p. 16–17; Mayol 2002, p. 221–222). Such rationales are hardly absent from municipal cultural policies in Canada but they do not, for the most part, figure prominently in their approach to cultural industries. One of the reasons why this might be so is the relatively clear separation of cultural industries policy and arts policy in Canada. All three levels of government in Canada have generally separated the two both in terms of administration and policy objectives and for the most part municipal government involvement has focused on the arts, indeed on high culture (Stanbridge 2007).

Paquette (2008, p. 299) describes the 'municipalisation' of cultural policy in Canada from the 1970s on as provincial governments devolved responsibility for culture to local authorities and, later, as local policy-makers began to view culture as a means for development. These ideas, typified by Richard Florida's account of the creative class (2002), have been taken up as enthusiastically by Canadian municipal policy-makers as those elsewhere. Cultural industries, however, (as opposed to arts and culture) have not been much utilised as instruments of local development by Canadian municipal governments. Paquette's research on local cultural policy development in Northern Ontario (2008, p. 306) finds that cultural industries are largely excluded from the process. *Montreal: Cultural Metropolis*, Montreal's cultural development strategy, refers to cultural industries as primarily the responsibility of federal and provincial governments (2005). There are of course the jurisdictional matters, as mentioned above, which preclude municipal involvement in issues directly relating to broadcasting, telecommunications, copyright or trade. Another important factor is that the large amounts of funding necessary for effective subsidy programmes for these industries are generally beyond the means of Canadian municipal governments.

None of this absolutely precludes any involvement with cultural industries on the part of municipal governments. Local authorities may involve themselves in cultural industries policy but by utilising a different set of instruments. Sancton (2012, p. 304) notes that, whilst there is a great deal of overlap and interaction between different levels of government on many policy matters, there is a general sense of what kinds of policies each level is best equipped to carry out. In Canada, he suggests, local governments are generally viewed as the appropriate venue for concerns with 'the regulation and servicing of property', such as 'zoning [and] local roads' (ibid.). Although such policies may not be able to address all aspects of the cultural industries' needs, it is clear that they may be able to carry out some kinds of policies that national programmes do not.

Perhaps the best example, and the exception that proves the rule in this case, is the large degree of involvement by municipal governments to pursue and enable film and television productions within their boundaries. Over the past several decades, a number of Canadian municipalities set up offices and commissions to encourage production companies to use their cities as locations for filming. 'Runaway' productions from Hollywood have been a considerable source of economic activity in Canadian cities, particularly Vancouver and Toronto. In Toronto alone in 2011, such American productions accounted for C\$530 million out of C\$1.13 billion (City of Toronto 2012). Provincial governments have also got in on the act, largely through tax incentives that make it attractive for companies to film in these areas and, in some cases, to fund infrastructure such as sound stages or post-production facilities. For city governments the policies have been different. For instance, cities can utilise their authority with respect to traffic management and zoning so as to allow for more convenience to producers. Cities utilise a set of nodal or information policies along two lines. First, they can promote themselves as attractive locations for production. Second, they can act as a liaison for producers, coordinating with other city departments or local private sector resources. This is generally done via film commissions or boards, set-up by municipal governments specifically for this purpose, separate from those bodies that administer local arts and cultural policy and with goals that are more purely economic.[3]

Whilst film offices and commissions are relatively common in Canadian cities, there are no music industry counterparts here and very few anywhere. The most notable example is Austin, Texas with its Music Commission and Division (Titan Music Group 2012), the result of a concerted effort involving the city's Chamber of Commerce, amongst others, which has forged links between the music sector and other prominent industries to develop infrastructure and to promote its music scene within the American entertainment industry (Shank 1994). The focus of Austin's music industry policy is mostly on live performance, which is also prominent in other examples of local music industry policy from Norwich to Melbourne. This is also consistent with Sancton's emphasis on the servicing and allocation of property as the proper sphere of local government. This further suggests that live entertainment may be the music industry sector where municipal policies can be most effective.

At the level of local policy, one of the most important distinctions between film and television production and live music is the degree to which the latter is embedded within other kinds of activities and industries, with the result that the most relevant policies for live music may not appear to be particularly concerned with music at all. Will Straw points to 'alcohol licensing laws, municipal zoning regulations, public performance regulations controlling the use of recorded music as entertainment, … agreements between nightclubs and local musicians' unions, and so on' (2005, p. 190–191) as important factors in contributing to the character and viability of Montreal's music scene. Very little of this would count as cultural policy per se. If this sometimes makes these policies difficult to identify as relevant, it makes it even more difficult for music industry concerns to prevail, as they are likely to conflict with other more powerful interests, such as those of local residents and businesses. To offer an extreme example, arguably, one of the major factors in Montreal's emergence as a highly publicised music scene early in the twenty-first century was the city's prolonged economic slump from the 1970s to the 1990s, which made it a relatively cheap place to live (Stahl 2001) – surely a path no policy-maker would deliberately follow!

The example provided by policies promoting film and television production also suggests that for Canadian municipal governments cultural industries policy must be justified largely on economic grounds. Where film and television production is concerned, there is a relatively easy case to make with considerable direct benefits to local economies. Film and television production activity in Toronto was worth \$1.13 billion in 2011 (City of Toronto 2012). However, as we shall see, the case is somewhat harder to make with some other cultural industries such as publishing or the music industry. The production costs for these industries are far less significant, which limits both their impact on a local economy and the need for production companies to seek out lower cost locations. If a case is to be made for municipal policy with respect to the economic impact of these industries then it must further identify the more indirect means by which this might occur. Nonetheless, it would appear municipalities and the policy-making apparatus associated with them (not only governments but also Chambers of Commerce and Economic Development Agencies) have the potential to play a substantial role in developing a more locally based industry, involving various approaches, ranging from incubation to promotion.

We now turn to discussion of our specific cases, each of which illustrates some common challenges but also very different situations. Calgary's policy presents perhaps the more involved history but Toronto offers us far better documentation of the state of the local music industry in its locale. Given that both concern efforts to bring the music industry into municipal policy, and given that neither has resulted in any substantial measures so far, they are nonetheless widely divergent in terms of how have played out. Much of this comes down to the very different group of actors involved in each case. Calgary, with its relatively small and isolated music industry, gained its initial impetus in City of Calgary agencies in the arts community. In Toronto's case, virtually all of the actors are from the industry, which is much larger and more developed.

Calgary. Music Lives Here[4]

Located in the province of Alberta in the western part of the country, Calgary is the fifth largest city in Canada with a population of roughly one million, which grew by 12.6% from 2006 to 2011 (Press 2012). It is a fairly affluent city, thanks in large part to its role as the corporate headquarters of much of Canada's oil and gas companies, with the highest average per capita income and the lowest unemployment rate in the country. The city is perhaps best known for the Stampede, its annual cowboy-culture celebration in early July, which marked its centenary in 2012. With all these advantages, Calgary is not a locale that springs to mind when one discusses Canada's centres of musical activity, which is not to say that the city is bereft of talented musicians – over the past decades a number of artists have emerged from Calgary, including Paul Brandt, Jann Arden and Feist. The city does face some particular challenges for the development of a local music industry. First, there is its relative isolation geographically – other than Edmonton the nearest major centre is Vancouver, 1000 kilometres west, across the Rocky Mountains, whilst Winnipeg is 1300 kilometres east. These distances are exacerbated by long, cold winters that make touring even more difficult. However, one of Calgary's biggest challenges is that it has become a very expensive place to live and to do business, especially for artists. These challenges are hardly unique – Vancouver has encountered similar difficulties in finding sustainable venues for emerging artists, as detailed in the documentary No Fun City (2010). Britain's live music scenes face these issues also (McVeigh and Bloodworth 2012). Nonetheless, whereas such locales start with some established reputation, Calgary is playing catch-up in this respect. It remains difficult to assess the economic significance of Calgary's music industry. There is still very little information available in terms of either its employment or economic impact (Calgary Economic Development 2012, p. 6).

For all these reasons, the announcement in November 2007 of the intention to create a policy intended to develop Calgary's popular music industry came as something of a surprise. This announcement was part of the lead up to Calgary hosting the 2008 Juno Awards (Canada's equivalent of the Grammy Awards) in April of that year. 'Calgary. Music Lives Here' was the slogan chosen by the Calgary's Host Committee for the 2008 Juno Awards but it was also, as co-chair of that committee and Calgary Arts Development President Terry Rock said, the brand for a legacy programme, an attempt to extract some kind of lasting impact from the event, much as the city's athletics had from the 1988 Winter Olympics (Personal Communication, Terry Rock 19 July 2010).

No other Canadian city had so clearly and publicly announced a commitment to building a strong local music scene and industry. The intention may have been bold but it quickly became evident that there was no concrete plan (or funding) for achieving this aim. Following the announcement, the Juno host committee charged Calgary Arts Development (or CADA, which oversees Calgary's arts programmes and policies) with forming a sub-committee made up of arts professionals in the city to recommend appropriate measures and to secure corporate donations to achieve them. The committee's advice was to 'promote the scene, get some resources to help get [artists] out of town, and do tours and showcases' (Learoyd 2008). To this end, it organised an industry showcase in Toronto in November 2007 for Calgary musicians. Rock's idea was, as he put it, to think of Calgary as a record label, a catchy phrase certainly (Personal Communication, Terry Rock 19 July 2010). But these ideas were all about branding and promotion of the city, to alert the rest of the country that Calgary actually has a music scene rather than the nuts and bolts of supporting and building one.

Over the next two years, CADA attempted to lay the foundation for this legacy. Its 2007–2008 Report, released not long after the Juno Awards took place, promised that they would have 'a lasting impact' and that they were 'working to bring new resources and stronger support structures to develop Calgary's growing music industry' (CADA 2008, p. 15). The 2008–2009 Report announced that a new not-for-profit organisation was 'in the early stages of formation with a mandate to provide resources and support to emerging and established music professionals in Calgary' (CADA 2009, p. 14) which indeed was the case. By the next year, the organisation changed its name to Music Calgary – the result of a trademark dispute with the Canadian Broadcasting Corporation's Hockey Night in Canada, which runs an annual contest between small towns called 'Hockey Lives Here'. More importantly, the organisation hired an Executive Director and officially launched in February 2010 with a number of announced aims.

> To further the development of professional Calgary musicians and the Calgary music community and foster greater exposure nationally and internationally; To promote and create programs advancing the education and economic viability of the Calgary music community/industry; To provide direction in professional development and training; To represent the Calgary music industry's interests to government and private sectors. (Music Calgary, 2011: http://musiccalgary.org/about/)

Since then the organisation has held several relatively small events in Calgary (including workshops with musicians and a couple of networking sessions), the last taking place in September 2011. To date, no lasting initiatives or concrete proposals have emerged – although it did hold showcase in Calgary over two nights in February 2013. For now, the emphasis of the organisation seems to have shifted to dialogue – although its future is in doubt due to a lack of sustainable funding (Personal Communication, Shawn Petsche 1 October 2012). There remains no music industry policy for the city of Calgary.

It would appear that part of the problem is that neither CADA nor Music Calgary is really equipped to develop policy in cultural industries. CADA is an arts organisation and its primary function is providing funding and support for high culture and not-for-profit cultural organisations. It does an excellent job of funding and also advocating on behalf of these organisations with city and provincial governments. But as outlined above, arts policy is different from cultural/creative industries policy. Industrial strategy is neither CADA's forte nor its mandate. Perhaps realising this, it handed responsibility to Music Calgary and to a few figures involved in Calgary's music businesses and organisations. But the latter organisation faces two challenges: first, it is new, small and under-resourced and second, its principal members are the not-for-profit arts organisations CADA funds. For the most part, these are presenters and festivals with which CADA dealt most directly. These organisations rely heavily on government funding and their emphasis, although they assist local talent to some extent, is on presenting bigger name acts from elsewhere. There has been a serious lack of involvement of either the private businesses involved in music in Calgary or policy agencies with a more economic and industrial focus.

Is there a need for such a policy? There are a number of other music-related initiatives in Calgary worth mentioning. Chief amongst these is the National Music Centre (formerly the Cantos Music Foundation), a plan for a major facility housing an extensive collection of musical instruments, a Canadian music hall of fame, as well as performance and rehearsal spaces, and some recording facilities. This $130 million centre, slated to open in 2015, has attracted considerable support from all three levels of government, including $25 million from the City of Calgary, which sees the Centre as a key element in its longstanding plan to redevelop the area of the city immediately east of the downtown and as part of its strategy for attracting tourists. The National Music Centre is certainly the marquee music-related project in the city. It should certainly be the cornerstone of an integrated plan for Calgary's music community but the foundation's concern is primarily with building its facility and it has no formal relationships with other music-related initiatives in Calgary at this point. Another very interesting music industry-related initiative is the City of Calgary's Arts and Culture Directorate's youth educational programmes, particularly 'Toast 'n' jam', which provides participants with professional guidance leading towards a live festival at the end of the summer, and including 'an Industry Weekend Conference' (City of Calgary 2012).

Again, it is the private sector of the music business that is missing from the city's various policies and programmes. Amongst the funding programmes and large-scale capital projects, there is little appreciation for the role that clubs, bars or small all-ages venues play in providing the infrastructure for a vital local music industry. A well conceived music industry strategy might have helped to bring this sector and its concerns to the table. This would involve ostensibly non-cultural policies, such as zoning, noise by-laws or business licences, all of which play a considerable role in determining which spaces may be used for performing music and how (Straw 2005).

To illustrate the consequences of such policies, just as Music Calgary was being launched, two stories about Calgary music venues broke in the local media. The first of these concerned the loss of one of the city's longest running clubs The Warehouse in late January 2010. A proposed change in its liquor licence from nightclub to private club did not match the zoning designation of its premises – local bands thus lost one of their most important venues (McCoy 2010). Only a month earlier, there was the near closure of an all-ages performance space The New Black Centre for Performing Arts, which also provided recording facilities and rehearsal space for local bands. The latter case arose because of zoning infractions, brought to the city's attention by one of the venue's neighbours (Sylvester 2010). With the intervention of their local city council representative, the New Black Centre was able to survive but another all-ages space started around the same time, Comrad Sound, was shut down by the city in the summer of 2010, again over questions of zoning and the nature of its business licence (Stewart 2010). In this case, another local council representative led the charge. Both venues complained that the city licensing process was confusing and arcane – there was no consistency in terms of the procedure. It would appear that these organisations could use the same sort of advocacy and guidance that the larger festivals have received from CADA.

The difficulties of the New Black Centre were particularly ironic because as one branch of the municipal government was attempting to shut them down, the facility had also been contracted by the Arts and Culture division to deliver one of its educational programmes. This is perhaps the most serious consequence of not having an overall strategy – a disconnect between various policies and programmes. An integrated policy along the lines of that developed by Melbourne would be enormously helpful in coordinating all the various initiatives with other aspects of municipal government so that they work in concert rather than in isolation or, indeed, at cross-purposes. This lack of coordination leads to situations such as the New Black Centre's, as well as conflicts between club and bar owners who at times see projects such as the National Music Centre and the Folk Festival's new venue as publicly subsidised competition. All this suggests that a music policy (one that includes the music industry and a somewhat wider frame of reference) to coordinate all of these initiatives might be a good idea.

Any strategy will require allies and resources from other non-musical, non-cultural sectors (one sees this in the comprehensive plan for Melbourne's Music Strategy (City of Melbourne 2010). In Calgary's case, the lead agency for the policy was unable to secure a wide enough coalition and the policy went nowhere as a result, suffering both from inadequate resources and a narrow constituency. But perhaps the biggest challenge to developing the policy, specific to Calgary, is its prosperity. It is not simply the issues of affluence referred to earlier but that prosperity tends to remove the impetus for developing an economically focused cultural industry policy in the first place. Calgary's privileged situation singularly undercuts many economic rationales, whether based on the need for development, diversification or employment. The energy industry and its attendant spin-offs have created a labour shortage, even amongst youth. In this circumstance, a cultural industry policy has less traction – perhaps another casualty of a 'petro-state' in which oil revenues discourage long-term economic diversification (Karl 1997, p. 222–242). Until the oil runs out, or governments make diversification a priority, this is unlikely to change. Music thus remains squarely the purview the concern of

POPULAR MUSIC AND CULTURAL POLICY

arts and culture policy. This is true, not only of Calgary, but all of Alberta, which funds arts relatively generously but which lacks any coordinated strategy for developing cultural industries. In any case, this situation may be the underlying cause both for a music industry policy emanating from the city's arts and culture agency and the initiative's lack of engagement with the more business-oriented aspects of music activity.

One promising sign is that Calgary Economic Development recently published its first Creative Industries Sector Profile (2012) and has announced plans for a state of the art production facility in the city, notably mobilising a broad coalition of key stakeholders in its approach to this project. However, its strategy remains focused on film and television. For the moment, 'Calgary. Music Lives Here' remains a unique foray into music business policy on the part of a Canadian city. The origins of the idea, as well as its ineffectiveness, speak to a policy environment in which, oddly enough, music is more likely to be valued for its own sake rather than for the economic activity it generates. Whilst this is the case, a music industry policy for the city remains elusive.

Toronto: leveraging the music industry

Toronto offers us a very different narrative from Calgary in almost every way. To begin with Toronto has considerable advantages over Calgary with respect to its music industry. With a population of 2.6 million (6 million in the Greater Toronto Area) (Titan Music Group 2012, p. 4), Toronto is Canada's largest city and its dominant financial and industrial centre. Unlike Calgary, it is within relatively easy reach of a number of other major centres in Canada and the United States. The city also enjoys a reputation as one of the most culturally diverse and vibrant locales in North America. Toronto is very much the centre of Canada's sound recording industry, accounting for 84% of the economic activity in the sector. It is also one of the largest live music markets in North America. Toronto can build on considerable strengths as leverage for a more integrated policy.

Whilst Alberta has few targeted programmes for cultural industries, and very little in the way of policy, Ontario has devoted considerable resources in this area. In contrast to Alberta, Ontario's cultural industries programmes, encompassing print, film and television, new media and music, are administered separately from arts funding, largely through the offices of the Ontario Media Development Corporation (OMDC), an arms-length government agency. Its Music Fund provides up to C$50,000 for sound recording projects (OMDC 2012a). This fund provided C$851,048 to the Ontario music industry in 2010–2011 (OMDC 2012b, p. 29) Music industry companies, including record labels, music publishers and management companies can also access OMDC's Export Fund for attendance at trade fairs and other such initiatives (OMDC 2012a). In addition, OMDC administers a 20% refundable tax credit for Canadian-owned, Ontario-based companies. This was worth a further $1.476 million to the Ontario music industry in 2010–2011 (OMDC 2012b, p. 16).

Another major difference from Calgary's case is the set of actors involved in policy development. Here, the initiative to develop a municipal music industry originated not with the city government or any of its agencies but with the music industry itself, with the June 2012 release of a detailed study and report *Accelerating Toronto's Music Industry Growth: Leveraging Best Practices from Austin,*

Texas. The study was funded by Music Canada, the trade association representing the Canadian sound recording industry, including Canadian divisions of the major multi-national labels. This is notable, given that the report is concerned primarily with the local live music scene. Music Canada, although clearly involved in Canadian music industry policy, represents its most globalised and arguably least Canadian component. The organisation's involvement in federal policies has been most prominent in the area of copyright. For obvious reasons, it has been far less involved in either Canadian content (although its members do record a reasonable number of Canadian artists, particularly the more successful ones) or in the subsidy programmes of the Sound Recording Development Program or its successor the Canada Music Fund, as its leading members, the major labels, are ineligible for this funding.

Austin-based consultants, Titan Music Group, were responsible for the report, which was announced at the Toronto music industry event North By Northeast, itself an affiliate of Austin's renowned South By Southwest, one of the major showcase and trade events on the international music industry's calendar. Although so far, there is no involvement from the City of Toronto, the proposal in many respects has everything that Calgary's initiative lacked – research on stakeholder's concerns, some hard numbers on the economic impact of the music industry, specific recommendations and, above all, an integrated vision of the music industry, encompassing a broad swathe of activities, including venues, recording studios and festivals, as well as record companies.

Using Austin's developed music industry initiatives as their model, the consultants offered a conception of the music industry that did not centre on sound recording. Indeed, that industry sounds only a minor note in the set of priorities and recommendations for local government. Instead, the report focuses primarily on live music as the area where local governments can have the most impact (Titan Music Group 2012, p. 25). The report discusses zoning and licensing issues for live music venues, stressing the need for consistent policies, coordination of government agencies and a role for government agencies in providing a forum for community engagement and consultation. In addition, the report identifies the need to promote Toronto's music industry. Here, again the emphasis is on live music. Whilst some of this involves attracting sound recording projects to local studios, the major thrust of the promotion is aimed at tourism, identifying the economic impact of music tourism and utilising or supplementing existing resources to make music more central to Toronto's tourism industry (Titan Music Group 2012, p. 93–95). Obviously, the major music attractions for tourists would involve opportunities to experience music performances at clubs, festivals or concerts.

A major thrust of the report is that its proposals should not be seen as arts policies but as economic policies. Moreover, the authors, for the most part, ground their rationale for support of Toronto's music industry in its direct contribution to economic activity rather than in terms of contributing to a more amenable environment for potential workers in other sectors. The report's 16 recommendations, mostly to the municipal government, generally focus on music as an industry in itself. Many of these recommendations involve setting benchmarks or further studying music's economic impact but some call for more immediate action. The first two recommendations in particular are noteworthy, building as they do on municipal involvement in the film industry as a model for music industry policy at this level of government. These recommendations are that the City of Toronto creates both a Music

Board to advise the city on music industry-related issues and that it create and fund a Music Office that coordinates policies and initiatives that help the industry (Titan Music Group 2012, p. 90). These initiatives resemble Austin's policies but they are even more similar to Toronto's existing policies for the film and television production industry.

In 2011, the Toronto Film and Television Office received C$1, 265, 400 in funding from the city (Titan Music Group 2012, p. 33). It returned approximately C$200,000 in direct revenues to the city through shooting permits but the indirect value of film production to the city was far greater, C$1.13 billion in 2011 (City of Toronto 2012). This presents a problem for the music industry. Toronto's share of Canada's sound recording industry activity is considerable at about C$260.7 million (Music Canada 2012, p. 24). This sector, however, (apart from recording studios) is not the focus of the report's recommendations. The numbers of recording studio revenues are much lower. In 2009, Ontario's recording studios had revenues of C$39.5 million in 2009, a decline of nearly 18% from the previous year (Titan Music Group 2012, p. 28). For the live music industry's revenues, the report's authors can only offer a figure for the country as a whole at C$455 million (Titan Music Group 2012, p. 27). Given that the live music industry is far less clustered in Toronto than the recording industry, the city's share of this number is likely to be only in the tens of millions.

On this basis, the music industry may have difficulty in commanding the same kind of attention and commitment from local government. Recording projects do not inject anything even approaching the amount of money into the local economy that audiovisual production does. Music may have some role in the C$4.6 billion tourism contributed to Toronto in 2011 (Canada News Wire 2012). However, given the overall revenues for live music across Canada, the economic value is likely to be relatively minor. In fact, on the evidence presented in the report itself, Toronto already has a relatively successful music industry by most standards. It seems unlikely that the government could leverage much more value out of it through these measures. Toronto's position within the Canadian music industry is unassailable. Given the distribution of Canada's population, it is hard to imagine that the headquarters of the major labels (the major source of economic activity for music in Toronto) would relocate to another part of the country. If, as the report suggests, Toronto is one of the top five markets for music in North America (Titan Music Group 2012, p. 4), then Toronto is already over-performing. The difficulty with importing Austin's initiatives for music industry development to Toronto may be that Toronto's music industry (and certainly its economy) does not really require them. Toronto's initiative then, for all that it has far more to build on than Calgary's, founders on the fact that the music industry does not offer enough in direct economic benefits to make it worth the kind of attention or investment that other industries receive from local governments in Canada.[5]

Conclusion: location is everything

It is too early perhaps to say just whether these cases will remain isolated, failed attempts or if they are the first, tentative steps towards a genuinely novel development in Canada's music industry policy. Both are in this sense novel and offer us a very different perspective on where Canadian music industry policy could have gone or might yet go, although there would, in the final analysis, appear to be little impetus for greater engagement between the music industry and local governments. Calgary's status as the only city to even attempt to deepen its involvement speaks to a general absence of the music industry as part of the municipal agenda in this country. Equally, that the 2012 report from Music Canada is the first call of any note from the Canada's music industry for greater municipal government involvement says much about how little local policies have been priorities for the industry. It is less surprising that this should come from the Toronto-based music industry. This too tells us something about how the industry is structured in Canada.

Based on its relative size and prominence, Toronto's local music industry is not so very far from being the national music industry, at least for English Canada.[6] Toronto already benefits more than any other location from existing federal music industry policies. The direct beneficiaries of these policies are, of course, the recording industry for the most part. Toronto's live music industry may also benefit indirectly, as the presence of more record labels, management companies and music publishers may act as a centre of attraction for artists and create extra opportunities for live performance. This is evident throughout the Titan Music Group report (2012), which repeatedly mentions the advantages conferred by them. Indeed, the report itself finds its genesis in the willingness of the recording industry to fund its creation. Calgary's music industry, on the other hand, is truly much more local, in terms of its isolation and its minor status. A music industry in Calgary cannot leverage such resources and must work that much harder to even define its policy object, which is evident in the vagueness of the proposal and its lack of consequences. Despite a willingness on the part of the city's arts agencies to entertain the possibility of a music industry policy, the industry itself remains too weak and fragmented to take-up its side in pressing for one. The result is a great disparity between these two cities, not so much in different kinds of policy instruments employed as, potentially at least, in the type of outcomes that could be expected, and above all, in the specific configuration of forces that would make a policy for the music industry a reality at the municipal level. Until this actually occurs, any policy analysis will have to wait to see precisely what that configuration is.

Notes

1. FACTOR, or the Foundation to Assist Canadian Talent on Record, is a private foundation that provides grants and loans for Canadian-owned music industry to produce recordings by Canadian artists. Some of the money comes from mandated contributions by Canadian broadcasters and the bulk of funding comes from the federal government under the New Works component of the Canada Music Fund.
2. In fact, some copyright policies, notably performing rights tariffs, may serve as more of a hindrance by imposing added costs on venues and promoters.
3. Nonetheless, as Tinic (2006, p. 156) has argued, they may have considerable benefits for local cultural production in terms of providing training and even infrastructure.
4. Much of the material on Calgary's attempted policy was garnered from a number of interviews conducted with policymakers and other prominent figures involved in Calgary's music scene between June 2010 and October 2012.
5. While the City of Toronto has not responded to the music industry's call for policies to promote live music, the Province of Ontario has, announcing the formation of a Live Music Working Group on 30 January 2013 to assist in developing a live music strategy for the province (Bliss 2013).
6. The Quebec based French Canadian music industry is in many respects a very different matter (Straw 2000).

References

Bliss, K., 30 January 2013. *Ontario government forms live music working group. Billboard* [online]. Available from: http://www.billboard.com/biz/articles/news/global/1536268/ontario-government-forms-live-music-working-group [Accessed 31 January 2013].

Calgary Arts Development Authority [CADA], 2008. *Annual report, 2007–2008.* Calgary: Calgary Arts Development Authority.

Calgary Arts Development Authority [CADA], 2009. *Annual report, 2008–2009.* Calgary: Calgary Arts Development Authority.

Calgary Arts Development Authority [CADA], 2012. *Calgary talent and innovation: creative industries sector profile.* Calgary: Calgary Economic Development.

Canada News Wire, 30 January 2012. *Media release: Toronto reaches milestone in tourism performance* [online]. Toronto. Available from: http://www.newswire.ca/en/story/912403/toronto-reaches-milestone-in-tourism-performance [Accessed 24 November 2012].

City of Calgary, 2012. *The city of Calgary – Toast 'n' jam* [online]. http://www.calgary.ca/CSPS/CNS/Pages/Children-and-youth/Toast-n-Jam/ToastJam.aspx [Accessed 8 June 2012].

City of Melbourne, 14 September 2010. *Future Melbourne (Economic development and knowledge city committee report) Agenda Item 5.4* [online]. Available from: http://www.melbourne.vic.gov.au/AboutCouncil/Meetings/Lists/CouncilMeetingAgendaItems/Attachments/8297/5.4.pdf [Accessed 24 May 2012].

City of Toronto, 2012. *Key industry sector: film and television* [online]. Available from: http://www1.toronto.ca/wps/portal/toronto/content?vgnextoid=5e46c1b5c62ca310VgnVCM10000071d60f89RCRD&vgnextchannel=de9819a575b6a310VgnVCM1000003dd60f89RCRD&vgnextfmt=default [Accessed 23 November 2012].

Federation of Canadian Municipalities, 2012. *The state of Canada's cities and communities 2012.* Ottawa: Federation of Canadian Municipalities.

Florida, R., 2002. *The rise of the creative class.* New York, NY: Basic Books.

Frith, S., 1993. Popular music and the local state. *In*: T. Bennett, S. Frith, L. Grossberg, J. Shepherd, and G. Turner, eds. *Rock and popular music: politics, policies, institutions.* London: Routledge, 14–24.

Gibson, C. and Homan, S., 2004. Urban redevelopment, live music and public space: cultural performance and the re-making of Marrickville. *International journal of cultural policy*, 10 (1), 67–84.

Homan, S., 2008. A portrait of the politician as a young pub rocker: live music venue reform in Australia. *Popular music*, 27 (2), 243–256.

Karl, T.L., 1997. *The paradox of plenty: oil booms and petro-states.* Berkeley, CA: University of California Press.

Lascoumes, P. and Le Galès, P., 2012. *Sociologies de l'action publiques* [The sociology of public action]. 2nd ed. Paris: Armand Colin.

Learoyd, M., 6 March 2008. *Music lives here, but is anyone listening? Fast forward weekly* [online]. Available from: http://www.ffwdweekly.com/article/music/music-features/music-lives-here-anyone-listening/ [Accessed 25 April 2010].

Malm, K. and Wallis, R., 1992. *Media policy & music activity.* London: Routledge.

Mayol, P., 2002. The policy of the city and cultural action. *Canadian journal of communication*, 27 (2–3), 221–229.

McCoy, H., 29 January 2010. *After-hour clubs lose liquor licence. Calgary Herald* [online]. Available from: http://www.calgaryherald.com/After+hours+clubs+lose+liquor+licence/2497900/story.html [Accessed 8 February 2010].

McVeigh, T. and Bloodworth, J., 26 May 2012. *Rock music under threat as small venues go bust across Britain. The Observer* [online]. Available from: http://www.guardian.co.uk/music/2012/may/26/rock-music-venues-bust-britain [Accessed 21 February 2013].

Miller, T. and Yúdice, G., 2002. *Cultural policy.* London: Sage.

Music Calgary, 2011. *About music Calgary* [online]. Available from: http://musiccalgary.org/about/ [Accessed 22 November 2011].

Music Canada, 2012. *Economic impact analysis of the sound recording industry in Canada.* Toronto: Music Canada.

No Fun City, 2010. *Film.* Vancouver, BC: Make Believe Media.

O'Brien, D. and Miles, S., 2010. Cultural policy as rhetoric and reality: a comparative analysis of policy making in the peripheral north of England. *Cultural Trends*, 19 (1/2), 3–43.

Ontario Media Development Corporation, 2012a. *OMDC – Music* [online]. Available from: http://www.omdc.on.ca/music.html [Accessed 24 November 2012].

Ontario Media Development Corporation, 2012b. *Annual report 2010–2011: supporting Ontario's Creative Industries* [online]. Available from: http://www.omdc.on.ca/AssetFactory.aspx?did=7548 [Accessed 24 November 2012].

Paquette, J., 2008. Engineering the Northern Bohemian: local cultural policies and governance in the creative city era. *Space and Polity*, 12 (3), 297–310.

Press, J., 8 February 2012. *Canada census 2011: the cities leading Canada's population boom. The national post* [online]. Available from: http://news.nationalpost.com/2012/02/08/canada-census-2011-see-which-cities-and-towns-have-grown-the-most/ [Accessed 11 June 2012].

Sancton, A., 2012. The urban agenda. *In*: H. Bakvis and G. Skogstad, eds. *Canadian federalism*. 3rd ed Toronto: Oxford University Press, 302–319.

Schön, D.A. and Rein, M., 1995. *Frame reflection: toward the resolution of intractable policy controversies*. New York, NY: Basic Books.

Shank, B., 1994. *Dissonant identities: the rock 'n' roll scene in Austin, Texas*. Hanover: Wesleyan University Press.

Shepherd, J., 1993. Value and power in music: an English Canadian perspective. *In*: V. Blundell, J. Shepherd, and I. Taylor, eds. *Relocating cultural studies: developments in theory and research*. London: Routledge, 171–206.

Shuker, R., 1994. *Understanding popular music*. London: Routledge.

Stahl, G., 2001. Tracing out an Anglo Bohemia musicmaking and myth in Montreal. *Public: cities/scenes*, 22/23, 99–121.

Stanbridge, A., 2007. The traditions of all the dead generations: music and cultural policy. *International journal of cultural policy*, 13 (3), 255–271.

Stewart, M.D., 24 June 2010. *Comrad sound facing closure. Fast forward weekly* [online]. Available from: http://www.ffwdweekly.com/article/music/music-features/comrad-sound-facing-closure-5903/ [Accessed 22 July 2010].

Straw, W., 1993. The English Canadian recording industry since 1970. *In*: T. Bennett, S. Frith, L. Grossberg, J. Shepherd, and G. Turner, eds. *Rock and popular music: politics, policies, institutions*. London: Routledge, 302–319.

Straw, W., 2000. In and around Canadian music. *Journal of Canadian studies*, 35 (3), 173–183.

Straw, W., 2005. Pathways of cultural movement. *In*: C. Andrew, M. Gattinger, M.S. Jeannotte, and W. Straw, eds. *Accounting for culture: thinking through cultural citizenship*. Ottawa: University of Ottawa Press, 183–197.

Street, J., 1993. Local differences? Popular music and the local state. *Popular music*, 12 (1), 43–55.

Sutherland, R., Forthcoming. Cancon and cold roads. *In*: G. Ross, G. Turnbull, and G. Whittall, eds. *Grassland sounds: popular and folk musics of the Canadian Prairies*.

Sylvester, K., 4 November 2009. *Why was punk rock booted? Metro* (Calgary ed.). *Reprinted on New Black Centre for Music and Art* [online]. Available from: http://www.thenewblackcentre.com/ [Accessed 16 November 2009].

Tinic, S., 2006. Global vistas and local reflections: negotiating place and identity in Vancouver television. *Television & new media*, 7 (2), 154–183.

Titan Music Group, 2012. *Accelerating Toronto's music industry growth: leveraging best practices from Austin, Texas*. Austin, TX: Titan Music Group.

Williamson, J. and Cloonan, M., 2007. Rethinking the music industry. *Popular music*, 26 (2), 305–322.

From Coombs to Crean: popular music and cultural policy in Australia

Shane Homan

ECPS, Monash University, Caulfield Victoria, Melbourne, Australia

The many bodies administering Australian arts activity were incorporated within the Australia Council, established in 1973 by the Whitlam Labor Government to oversee Commonwealth arts policy under the direction of H.C. 'Nugget' Coombs. This article takes the establishment of the Australia Council as a starting point in tracing changing attitudes towards the practices and funding of popular music in Australia and accompanying policy discourses. This includes consideration of how funding models reinforce understandings of 'high' and 'low' art forms, the 'cultural'/'creative' industries debates, and their effects upon local popular music policy. This article discusses the history of local music content debates as a central instrument of popular music policy and examines the implications for cultural nationalism in light of a recent series of media and cultural reports into industries and funding bodies. In documenting a broad shift from cultural to industrial policy narratives, the article examines a central question: What does the 'national' now mean in contemporary music and the rapid evolution of digital media technologies?

Introduction

Australasian artists such as The Seekers, The Bee Gees, Frank Ifield, The Easybeats, John Rowles and Rolf Harris have achieved international success. The forecast growth of the music industry in Australasia … should parallel the great expansion of growth predicted by the leaders of the industry and closely related to the enormous investment and talent which is available to bring about an expanded acceptance by the world's people of the pleasure available to them through the media of music. (Frederick C. Marks, Festival Records, Australia and New Zealand delegate cited in Marks 1969, p. 230)

At the First International Music Industry Conference held at Paradise Island, Nassau in 1969, the Australia–New Zealand delegate reported that the combined markets will 'parallel the great expansion and growth predicted by the leaders of the industry … the enormous investment and talent which is available to bring about an expanded acceptance by the world's people' of Australian and New Zealand music (ibid.). This optimism, however, was tempered by complaints that remain familiar to contemporary industry practitioners: the large distances from other key markets;

the small population sizes of both nations; the intrusion of government in terms of tax, trade and public broadcasting policies; and the high costs of production and distribution (ibid., p. 233–235). In this article, I want to undertake a basic mapping of the place of popular music in Australia, and how understandings of both the industrial and the cultural have in turn informed national policy settings. The re-examination of policy history, the settled ways of policy formation and under-standings of cultural activity are always useful in identifying how cultural forms (in this case popular music) are considered as part of the national furniture – or not. I'm also considering histories here because I argue that the settled ways of doing things are increasingly under challenge. There has been considerable policy activity in Australia in recent times: the *Strategic Contemporary Music Industry Plan* (2010), the *National Digital Economy Strategy* (2011), the *Convergence Review* (2012), a *Review of the Australia Council* (Trainor and James 2012) and the drafting of the much delayed *National Cultural Policy*, scheduled for release in late March 2012. This policy collection, in train since 2009, shares a preoccupation with how the arts, cultural and media economies confront an increasingly sophisticated digital economy. They also provide some new directions for how contemporary governments conceive of 'the national'.

Before addressing this recent activity, further historical context is presented in order to appreciate the more recent policy discourses and shifts. In this sense, the article traverses the arts/cultural policy terrain from the time of H.C. 'Nugget' Coombs, the first chairman of the Australia Council for the Arts, to the current federal Arts Minister, the veteran Labor[1] Party MP, Simon Crean. This brief history is important in understanding how Australian popular music policy was originally formed, and how important recent policy and industry shifts might be.[2]

Policy construction sites

The Australia Council for the Arts, established in 1968 and granted statutory authority in 1975, is the starting point here, as a body that enjoyed largely biparti-san support. It was created during the Gorton conservative[3] federal government in the late 1960s, with substantial budgetary increases from 1973 to 1975 under the Whitlam Labor government. The conservative federal governments of the 1950s and 60s attempted to create a range of 'quality' arts productions modelled upon British arrangements and institutions (e.g. the Elizabethan Theatre Trust in 1954, the Australian Opera Company in 1956, the Australian Ballet company in 1962). However, Australian youth voted with their (dancing) feet and embraced the arrival of teen cinema and rock and roll. By the late 1960s, film was considered suffi-ciently important as a national cultural form to receive significant infrastructure funding with the establishment of the Australian Film Development Corporation in 1970 by the Gorton federal government.

Until the 1970s, the 'high' arts (opera, classical music, music theatre) were the only music forms considered for public funding, reflected in the initial arts bodies discussed above. No better example of the habitual linkage of 'the Arts' with high culture exists than the 1971 announcement by the conservative Prime Minister William McMahon of a 17% increase in funding to these forms: 'those who love the arts will rejoice that Australian Opera has been given an effective opportunity to set new standards of excellence' (cited in Rowse 1985, p. 32). The distinction between 'entertainment' and 'high' cultural forms was established early on by Coombs upon his appointment to the Australia Council (ibid., p. 35). As Tim Rowse has explained, Coombs acknowledged a fundamental problem at the core of funding debates of 'achieving a proper balance ... between the promotion of excellence and the widening of participation in and experience of the arts' (cited in Guldberg 2000, p. 97). The competing aims of 'excellence' and access/participation – and whether they were mutually exclusive – came to the fore in arts policies of the Whitlam Labor government's brief tenure in office from 1972 to 1975. The Australia Council's music board funded community music projects, including musicians-in-residence and community music development workers (Costello 2003, p. 159).

Industries Assistance Commission (IAC)

> Chairman: Do you think the reasons governments do not give assistance to rock and roll, for instance, is that the people who are handing out the money do not consider rock and roll to be art?

> Mr. Meldrum: Absolutely. I think the myth of going back to the days when rock and roll was under the guise of sex, drugs and rock and roll is quite absurd now. Over the last 10 years especially, rock and roll has proved to be a very professional business. (TV/recording producer Ian 'Molly' Meldrum at IAC hearings, 4 November 1985, cited in Breen 1999, p. 97)

The beginnings of a shift in broader thinking about the non-flagship arts can be seen in the controversial Industries Assistance Commission of 1976, a report that was 'commissioned by [Prime Minister] Whitlam, hijacked by the hardliners in the IAC, and presented to an unsympathetic [subsequent Prime Minister] Fraser' (Craik 2007, p. 11). The Commission's remit was broad in examining federal government structures and industries to maximise efficiency and use of national resources. The role of existing tariffs and other protectionist policies was a particular focus, but also areas where the government could provide further assistance to local industries. In contrast to the overriding tone of the report demanding 'structural adjustment' for those industries which had enjoyed tariff and other trade protections, the music industries were highlighted as deserving to receive 'low levels of assistance' in the forms of 'facilitation of access to overseas markets, and provision of assistance for innovation and research' (Commonwealth of Australia 2003, p. 28). A succession of music industry figures submitted evidence to the IAC, including the first major local success story of 1950s Australian rock and roll, Johnny O'Keefe, who argued for a $1.5 million music industry grant, and the increase in local content laws (see below for an outline of the introduction of music radio quotas) for broadcasting to a symbolic 33 and 1/3% (the speed at which vinyl albums are played) (Breen 1999, p. 175, Johnstone 2001, p. 279).

The Australia Council and the arts communities hoped for Commission recommendations of increased high arts subsidies. Instead, the arts communities and the government got more than they bargained for. The IAC adopted the view that 'culture' 'in broad terms, [is] the expression of a community's way of life' (cited in Gibson 2001, p. 78). It recommended to reduce, and indeed phase out, direct funding of the major arts companies over a five-year period, with support to be redirected to arts activities that emphasised innovation, education and community objectives. The Fraser government quickly distanced itself from the Commission findings, with the Prime Minister stating that 'art is not something which can be judged merely by harsh economic criteria' (ibid., p. 79). This reflected the many difficulties that a conservative coalition government faced in terms of industry reform that involved 'structural adjustment', not the least Fraser's own inclination to 'instrumental protectionism' (Glezer cited in Commonwealth of Australia 2003, p. 37). This, of course, extended to arts policies, where a decision to leave the flagship companies to market forces was indefensible, particularly given the government's trusted recourse to 'excellence' arguments that had existed alongside its free market rationales since the 1940s.

Whilst it did not change the central policy discourse – 'the Arts' were still considered to be a special fiscal case – the IAC did establish a beachhead for later debates about arts and culture, and industry and subsidy forms. In 1983, the Australia Council published *The Artist in Australia Today* by David Throsby (Australia Council 1983). It found that rock and pop performers consisted of 38.7% of its research interview sample, a sizeable number given that these artists were not considered for assistance within Australia Council funding (Rowse 1985, p. 84). The 1984/85 report of the Australia Council Music Board reported that $55,385 was allocated to popular music; in effect, one-seven-hundredth of the Australia Council's total budget (Gillard 1990, p. 21).

In the wake of the IAC insistence that the arts be considered along a spectrum of industries for government assistance, a further report was commissioned. The House of Representatives' report *Patronage, Power and the Muse: Inquiry into Commonwealth Assistance to the Arts* (commonly known as the McLeay report after its Labor chair, Leo McLeay) was delivered in 1986. Its brief was to define the role of government according to different artistic activity. Importantly, it placed the high arts on notice: 'it rejected "the view that Commonwealth assistance is a right of the arts because of their merits"' (Craik 2007, p. 92). This was in keeping with the inquiry's acknowledgement that 'cultural value is not limited to any narrow range of activities' (Breen 1999, p. 101). In terms of assistance to forms of 'new art' (contemporary, mainstream cultural activity), access and diversity were principal objectives. Support for contemporary popular music was more feasible then, within these parameters, and the McLeay report recommended training, education and recording assistance, along with a blank tape levy to fund Australian composers (Breen 1999, p. 101–102).

Policy action

By the late 1980s, the IAC and McLeay reports had transposed into some effort to understand the scope of the popular music sector. *The Australian Music Industry: An Economic Evaluation* report (Australia Council 1987, p. 1) finally provided evidence of its domestic and international worth, arguing that the local music industry was comparable to the clothing, textile and footwear industries in size and income – but without the accompanying subsidies. There was also movement elsewhere. In a rare acknowledgement of the continuing power of the high arts lobby, New Zealand Prime Minister David Lange pointed out in 1986 that successful local pop groups attracted wider audiences without government subsidies, in favourable comparison to the expensive, but less heard, national symphony orchestra (Shuker 2003, p. 244).

The combination of industry research reports translated to federal government agreement that a music assistance body be organised, to be funded by a levy on blank tapes (Breen 1999, p. 104). Established in 1988, Ausmusic was designed to provide training schemes, performance events and advice to government on contemporary music matters. Its effectiveness was later constrained by conflicting rationales and funding (separate to market forces, yet funded by sponsors like Coca Cola) and as a body that did not have the full support of the industry. Further, in the absence of a levy on blank cassette tape sales, government funding was eventually withdrawn.[4]

Yet the 1980s do represent a shift, especially after the demise of the Fraser government, and the election of Labor in 1983. Whilst patronage strategies remained, Craik has argued that this era also incorporated 'architect' strategies (Craik 2007, p. 13), with reports commissioned across youth arts, orchestras, indigenous arts and cultural employment (against a backdrop of broader deregulation of the media industries and related preoccupations with media ownership). With a Labor Prime Minister, Bob Hawke, fond of sport and the race track and a Labor Treasurer, Paul Keating, who had been a rock band manager in his youth, the case began to be made for rock music to be viewed as an indisputable source of nationalism, in a similar way to sport, with Australians to collectively share in its triumphs, as leisure forms that uphold the egalitarian myth of Australian life. In economists' terms, music, like sport activity, brought 'external benefits' beyond those who play music and sport.

Nationalist discourses can, of course, be used to mask specialised interests (Turner 1994, p. 159). The undeniable claims of pub rock as an essential form of Australian youth culture in the 1970s and 80s, for example, became evident in its wider, colloquial classification as 'Oz Rock' (Homan 2008), even as it disguised its exclusion of other music genres and identities of equal importance to multicultural Australia (Brophy 1987). With the exception of Aboriginal rock (a fusion of rock forms and indigenous sounds and song writing), Australian rock and pop musicians cannot lay claim to a unique national sound or genre. Yet by the early 1980s, a combination of industry stakeholders and politicians laid claim to popular music as intrinsic to Australian life. This was reinforced by older value judgments based on gender and genre, and between 'serious' rock and 'lightweight' pop (Frith 1996). For example, Kylie Minogue's initial local career was disrupted by mainstream commercial music radio's refusal to play her songs amidst accusations that she produced 'lightweight' pop and did not emerge from the beery pub rock circuits of the main Australian cities (Rex 1992).

The Hawke Labor government incorporated rock music within its export strategies, based upon the success of acts such as Midnight Oil, Icehouse, Men At Work and others in the U.S. and Europe (Breen 1999, p. 75). Beyond the directions and effects of policy decisions, the influence of particular individuals – for better or worse – cannot be underestimated. The role of self-appointed 'champions' and their more informal music industry networks were crucial to changing government attitudes and policy. The role of popular music funding in the *realpolitik* of the Australian electorate also cannot be dismissed; popular music was perceived as a means for politicians, particularly those in the federal Labor government of the 1980s, to connect with youth and secure their vote (Breen 1999, p. 52–53).

The Keating Labor government's *Creative Nation* (1994) report can perhaps be regarded as a symbolic high point in the acknowledgement of popular music (and other non-traditional cultural sectors). It aspired to a whole-of-government approach previously lacking in other arts policies, linking cultural delivery and content mechanisms, the communications and arts portfolios, with Arts placed for the first time in Cabinet. New initiatives were established, such as the *Playing Australia* touring programme for musicians. More significantly, the policy document stated that:

> Music has always formed an important part of Australians' lives, whether through listening to the radio, home entertainment, or a concert performance ... Australian contemporary[5] music is a significant contributor to the Australian economy with a turnover of approximately $1.5 billion annually. (Commonwealth of Australia 1994, p. 25, 29)

Here, popular music contributes to both the cultural and the *economic* well being of the nation. This important rider – its contribution to national Gross Domestic Product – accompanied Prime Ministerial interest in popular music, with the music press making much of Keating's teenage stint as band manager. This was reflected in continued funding of Ausmusic (1994) training and research programmes (for example, its *Stayin' Alive* reports on the health of live music); and the national advisory body, MIAC (the Music Industry Advisory Council). Despite common presumptions that Labor was the natural party of arts constituencies, and delivered policies accordingly, its policy history reveals a mixed landscape of confused priorities. Deregulation of the radio and television industries, and accompanying reductions in profit margins, led to instability and less local content (see Turner 2001). Don Watson's take on his time as an advisor to Keating as Prime Minister is instructive, for his descriptions of how Keating detested dealing with the arts communities, with the belief that they could never be satisfied (see Watson 2002).

Nonetheless, *Creative Nation* provided additional funding for the usual arts channels and retained support for 'excellence' and the flagship arts companies. Yet, it also created a new emphasis upon multimedia forms and began some initial thinking about the implications for copyright, for example, in digital economies. This signalled a shift from emphases on the cultural producer, to visible audience demand for cultural forms (Radbourne 1997). Interestingly, at the same time, the conservative Opposition, led by John Hewson, produced an arts policy that included less centralised power of subsidy by the Australia Council, and returning non-flagship arts activity and funding to the States (Craik 2007, p. 15).

I have already mentioned the failure of the Labor federal government to establish a blank tape levy as a major funding source for contemporary music in 1993. The most evident tension between the Labor governments' preference for deregulated cultural industries participating in a diverse and mobile global economy, and older nationalist sentiments about domestic production, was to be found in the debates about the Prices Surveillance Authority (PSA) findings into the prices of CDs.

The PSA *Inquiry into the Price of Sound Recordings* revealed 'the private, invisible hand of copyright law in regulating the interests of the major record companies by maintaining their monopoly over product distribution' (Breen 1999, p. 176). The PSA concluded that, due to the absence of domestic price competition and protection from imports afforded by the Copyright Act, Australian consumers paid excessive prices for CDs in comparison with other countries. The report's primary recommendation consisted of weakening the multinationals' dominance by removing their local subsidiaries' exclusive licence agreements for CDs within Australia. This was to be achieved by allowing non-pirate CDs, that is, those manufactured legitimately under licence of the copyright owner, to be imported without requiring the consent of the Australian copyright owner. After commissioning the report, the Keating Labor government refused to implement parallel importing, after intensive protests from the music industry. Acknowledging the decline in local artist investment that was highlighted in the PSA report, the industry promised $270 million for local development (Rowe 2001, p. 52).

The debate to this point had been drawn upon familiar cultural industry lines: that copyright deregulation/competition would destroy the 'fragile' local industry, and the impetus for local production (see Homan 1999, Rowe 2001). The industry argued that copyright was not merely a contractual mechanism in the interests of the artist, but the primary means by which the recording companies establish their wealth through territorial exploitation of publishing rights. However, the election of the conservative Howard Coalition government in 1996 signalled a shift from traditional industry protection arguments (where multinational investment and distribution remains at the core of 'local' music production), to that of consumer rights. The copyright amendments to enable parallel imports became law in July 1998.

The withdrawal of Ausmusic's $1.2 m funding in 1996 by the Howard government, the loss of the High Court case that ruled blank tapes to be unconstitutional, the introduction of parallel importing and the industry's subsequent withdrawal of its promise of its $270 m investment in local artists certainly signalled a changed landscape. With the exception of broadcasting content policies (discussed below), this defined the end of the 'policy moment' (Breen 1999, p. 22) for popular music that began in the early 1980s.[6]

Arts to cultural to creative industries

The other key driver of the debate has been the shift from 'arts' to 'cultural' or 'creative' industries, evident on two broad fronts. Firstly, the Blair Labour government's policy directions for 'the arts' in 1998 (Smith 1998) in Britain are broadly understood as the foundational moment for cultural/creative industry policy, where the connections between culture and the economy were made even more explicitly than in *Creative Nation*. Under Blair, the direction of greater governmental resources to the 'creative industries' was a means of connecting its themes of individualism and enterprise with the booming design, fashion, media, sport, theatre, advertising and software industries. Popular music's prominent place at the government table was no doubt helped by the 'Cool Britannia' period of high pop exports, a Prime Minister who had been a rock lead singer in his university days, and the Blair cabinet's eagerness to be the fashionable party of youth (see Harris 2003). This translated to significant programmes, including the Youth Music programme to fund local government and school hubs of music activity.

Secondly, Richard Florida's definition of the 'creative industries' (2002, 2007) and his ranking of cities by a creativity index has been both influential and controversial. Criticisms include the difficulty in measuring economic impact; the limits of creative industries policy templates that do not account for local or regional difference (Gibson and Klocker 2005); the potential for exploitation of creative labour (McRobbie 2002, Hesmondhalgh and Baker 2011); and that understandings of 'creativity' and 'culture' are based increasingly upon discourses of economic benefit rather than artistic and public good (e.g. McGuigan 2005). The 'Florida effect' has been keenly felt in Australia; even small towns have a creative/cultural city plan based to differing extents on the Florida model, whilst the larger capital cities construct theirs with an eye to regional and global competition. And music has been central. The irony is not lost on musicians reading glossy state documents proclaiming a 'cultural and creative city' (City of Sydney 2008) that continues to ignore the adverse effects of gentrification upon the ability of musicians to not only afford to live within CBDs, but its adverse effects in relation to noise complaints, and the higher land values which have seen some iconic venues sold for other commercial purposes. State music bodies such as Music Victoria and Music NSW are also drawing attention to other policies, including the need for coordinated late night transport, parking allowances for musicians loading into venues and declining state support for local music festivals. At the same time, the need for a coordinated *national* set of policies and aims remains. The 2005 report *Let's Get The Show on the Road* outlined the obstacles to a 'cohesive contemporary industry', emphasising the lack of coordination between states, and a 'highly fragmented' music sector that was failing to present a unified voice to government (Allen Consulting Group 2005, p. v–vi, see also Cloonan 2008). The range of competing issues – and separate interests – is still evident in contemporary policy arguments and practices. However, as discussed below, some debates have managed to unify popular music practitioners.

Cultural to industrial?

I've briefly traced here how simpler notions of 'the arts' have become complicated in the past 20 years, particularly as the cultural is increasingly called upon to pull its weight as part of GDP considerations. In this final section, I want to flag some of the more recent challenges to understandings of the arts and culture in Australian life.

In the absence of direct assistance, the most explicit acknowledgement of Australian popular music as a cultural form has existed in the long history of content quotas for broadcasting. In 1942, the first local music content quota (2.5%) was established to ensure that radio airplay was not totally dominated by North American and European artists. In 1976, the quota for Australian radio was increased from 10 to 20%, with the Labor Whitlam government granting 12 public radio licences a year earlier (4ZZZ in Brisbane, 2XX in Canberra, 5MMM in Adelaide, 2JJ in Sydney and 3RRR in Melbourne). These were important steps in the formation of newer youth audiences prepared to buy local recordings and see local performers. In 1992, quotas were established according to music genre: stations playing commercial rock and pop had to ensure that 25% of material was from Australian artists. Since October 1999, at least 25% of Australian musics played by mainstream rock and contemporary hits stations must be material released in the past year (Commercial Radio Codes of Practice, ABA, 2000). This ensured that contemporary acts were included within the commercial stations' diet of 'hits and memories'. The content quotas have been invaluable in ensuring that domestic musicians and composers are heard on broadcasting formats that privilege international artists. This has entailed a social contract of sorts, with both industry and

POPULAR MUSIC AND CULTURAL POLICY

government agreed on the need for intervention on behalf of the local product. These broad agreements are in question on a range of fronts.

Firstly, the role of broadcasting is increasingly under question. The uneasy relationship between the radio and recording company sectors has broken into open warfare in recent years. In 2011, the central collection society of broadcasting royalties for musicians, the Phonographic Performance Company of Australia (PPCA), lodged with the High Court of Australia an application to lift the 1% cap on radio broadcasting royalties established in 1969, citing much higher rates paid by the radio sector in other national markets, and the current rate's disproportionate share related to the heavy lifting done by music across formats (see PPCA 2011). A High Court ruling in March 2012 found in favour of the broadcasters, and the 1% cap has remained (see Australian Copyright Council 2012). It was not surprising that the PPCA action seeking a higher royalty rate inflamed the commercial radio sector. Commercial Radio Australia's Joan Warner stated that:

> If something happens to the 1 per cent cap because it's supposedly an unfair acquisition, what about the music quota which is forced supply of a product? ... Is there unfair acquisition of our only product, which is air time, by a forced supply from a particular group of music companies? (cited in Sexton 2010)

This placed Commercial Radio Australia at odds with its previous commitments. As stated within the commercial radio sector's 'Code of Practice 4' of the *Broadcasting Services Act 1992*:

> The commercial radio industry is committed to supporting the music of Australian artists and composers ... [it] will continue to encourage the increased production by the record industry of Australian music relevant to stations formats and the preferences of the Australian listening public. (ACMA 2011)

For the first time since 1942, the worth – and mutual benefits – of radio content quotas was openly discussed. Undeterred, the PPCA instigated new legal proceedings challenging the royalty contexts of streamed broadcasting, and the right of commercial broadcasters to simulcast recordings on the internet at the same time as their AM, FM and digital radio broadcasts. At issue was the definition of 'broadcast' within the industry agreement between stations and the copyright society. In February 2012, the Federal Court ruled that:

> ... the simulcast transmission of the same radio program via the FM waves and the Internet is also a 'broadcast' within [the definition] of the Copyright Act and, for that reason, is within the scope of the licence which PPCA agreed to grant to the members of CRA and which it did grant from time to time to members of CRA [within the terms of their agreements]. (Justice Foster, Federal Court of Australia, cited in Catania 2012)

The PPCA did not accept that simulcasts were within the scope of the original agreements and appealed the decision. In February 2013, the full bench of the Federal Court overturned its previous ruling, indicating that 'the delivery of the radio program by transmission from a terrestrial transmitter is a different broadcasting service from the delivery of the same radio program using the internet' (Phonographic Performance Company of Australia Limited v Commercial Radio

Australia Limited 2013). If no further appeals are lodged by Commercial Radio Australia, the full bench judgment clears the way for an internet streaming tariff to be applied to recordings protected within the Australian *Copyright Act*. Apart from its argument that internet royalties would simply bring Australia into line with similar royalty streams overseas, the collection societies and recording companies also made clear its intentions to closely observe other digital consumption areas as future income growth streams: 'as the range of devices increases, listening audiences and revenue opportunities are growing ... it is important that artists and labels receive a fair share' (PPCA CEO Dan Rosen cited in PPCA 2013).

Secondly, the music quota question was revisited in the recent Convergence Review. Its Interim Report noted submissions from both sides for the removal of media content quotas and their maintenance. In its final report, delivered in March 2012, the Review recommended keeping the existing quotas and looking to extend them to digital broadcasting landscapes and soundscapes:

> The Review considered Australian music quotas on analog commercial radio. The Review found that the quotas are generally effective and recommends that they apply to content service enterprises that offer both analog and digital commercial radio services. Occasional or temporary digital radio services should be exempted from this requirement. The diversity and emerging nature of internet-delivered audio services would make it difficult and ineffective to apply quotas to these services at this time. (Commonwealth of Australia 2012, p. xii)

The Review considered a range of regulatory issues, from classification to media ownership, and argued the need for a new national regulator that could apply expertise and governance across all forms of content production and consumption. Its primary innovation lay in the classification and obligations of 'content service enterprises', the larger cultural and media organisations that produce 'professional content' (ix). Removing traditional broadcasting licence fees, these organisations would instead contribute to a 'converged content production fund' that would ensure the production of traditional and new local content. The fund could 'play a role in supporting Australian contemporary music' in particular (ibid., p. xii). The Review acknowledged the need to retain the existing content quotas for commercial radio, reinforcing the report's submissions on Australian consumers' continued preference for Australian programming. Yet it believed that 'given the evolving state of internet-based music services, quotas should not be applied at this time' (ibid., p. xix); it also recommended against Australian content quotas for the rapidly expanding free to air digital television channels. Quotas were to be considered once digital and internet radio had matured (ibid., p. 77).[7] Overall, both television and radio would be obliged to observe content quotas as a condition of their spectrum licence (ibid., p. 82).

Apart from introducing content quotas for the new digital television channels (and in turn extending the tax rebate on the networks for implementation of their digital offerings), the current Gillard Labor government has not produced any meaningful response to the rest of the Review's recommendations across ownership, production, distribution or regulation. This is symptomatic of a minority government with a looming election; but it may also speak to the sheer array of issues that the report canvassed, and the number of debates it left unsettled. For example, 'While it may seem reasonable to assume that media companies that are required to fund production will make that content available, it is no longer certain that

Australian content will be widely distributed, or that current volumes will be maintained, let alone increased' (Goldsmith 2012). Further, its 'content service enterprise' definition, crucial to local production obligations, does not cover some of the largest multi-platform providers on the Australian landscape: Telstra, Google, Apple and Facebook amongst many others.

The Review is part of a gradual but persistent trend to national governments grappling with new media and cultural landscapes with interlocking problems, chiefly the increasing divergence of production and consumption sites, and the multiplicity of producers that transcend national boundaries and lines of consciousness (cf. recent calls for the Australian federal government to investigate the local tax contributions of the multinationals (Hall 2012); and a parliamentary inquiry into Australian prices of global digital technology, including digital/streamed music (Peatling and O'Rourke 2012). The 'quota question' is relevant here in witnessing a decline in direct enforcement of local content, and more complex means of 'encouraging' local production. This is in keeping with the view, evident in the many submissions by the larger media empires to the various media and cultural policy reviews in the last two years, that local quotas are increasingly meaningless in an era of digital abundance and global consumerism. This shift also sees an emerging emphasis upon not protecting Australian content but boosting its quantity and visibility on media platforms. The Rudd Labor government's Arts Minister, Peter Garrett, expressed an intent to 'encourage ongoing exposure and increased diversity of Australian contemporary music across various platforms' (Commonwealth of Australia 2010, p. 12). The 2010 *Strategic Contemporary Music Industry Plan* discussion paper also sought views on 'financial support to assist new and emerging artists and bands to produce broadcast-ready, and commercially viable, products for radio' (ibid.).

Funding challenges

As explained at the start of this article, Australian policy-makers directly transplanted the intent and structures of British arts policy as much as possible, with the Australia Council for the Arts as its dominant funding body. Criticisms of the Council's funding allocations have been made at various times (e.g. Johnson 1995), however, recent critiques have more directly confronted 'excellence'/'popular' divisions. Indeed, the existence of the Australia Council as the nation's primary gatekeeper of arts and culture is increasingly open to debate. The Labor Arts Minister who succeeded Peter Garrett, Simon Crean, announced a review of the Council in December 2011. The report delivered to the Minister in May 2012 (Trainor and James 2012) maintained its emphasis upon 'excellence', with some new contingencies. Comparisons of arts funding as a percentage of GDP were not flattering: both Canada (0.156%) and New Zealand (0.198%) spent more than Australia (0.084%) (ibid., p. 22). Retaining the major support for its flagship companies, the report recommended a new funding stream of $15b for 'unfunded excellence' (ibid.). Amongst a range of options to diversify funding, the report acknowledged 'a level of outrage' about a 'perceived imbalance in funding towards other more traditional musical genres namely opera and orchestral music' (ibid., p. 35). A portion of the outrage became evident in the series of dissections of Council funding by cultural commentators (Eltham 2010, Westbury 2010). Similarly, in his submission to the National Cultural Policy discussion paper, live music advocate John Wardle pointed out that:

The Australia Council invested $83.5 million in music in 2011, of which only $5.3 million goes to the Music Board and not all of that to contemporary music. This needs to be increased by at least $5 million targeted at contemporary music industry development. (Wardle 2011)

The funding debate was further inflamed in 2012 with Minister Crean's decision to end the funding of Melba Records, the classical music recording company which has received $7.25 m since 2004 directly from the federal government. The Howard government's initial decision to separately fund a classical recording company outside the purview of the Australia Council created much anger within the popular music community, which perceived older notions of 'excellence' being directly applied and supported without due process, whereby one label received assistance though Ministerial fiat (see Australia Council 2012, Eltham 2012).

What becomes of the national?

In this article, I have charted the progression of Australian cultural policy as it has related to popular music. In one sense, its history is very similar to that of other developed Western nations in terms of the central, competing discourses. In another, it is a history of accompanying political party platforms, of conservative governments' default instincts to 'excellence', and centre-left government tendencies to speak of culture in national/economic terms. Clearly, decisions about which cultural forms were/are to be funded speak to underlying assumptions about 'quality' works and traditions. Historically, those music forms (opera and classical concerts) with the lowest participation rates have received the larger portion of subsidy; whilst those with the highest participation rates (rock and pop) have received little. Indeed, consistent arguments have been made that Australia Council funding in particular confers cultural status on particular artists and art forms; that 'funding and a reputation for excellence define each other' (Rowse 1985, p. 34). It is not surprising that 'excellence' discourses have taken so long to be actively questioned, particularly in relation to effects upon funding decisions, when the deep roots of such discourses are considered (see Street 2012).

In addition, relationships between cultural and media producers were predicated upon the sense of a 'cultural' or 'national' hearth delivered through public broadcasting. Government intervention has primarily been in the name of 'telling Australian stories', and the popular music industries have attempted to match film in this respect since the 1980s. For the classical music industry, government intervention has been in the name of 'excellence' and market failure. Both forms have been part of cultural policy directed at explicit nation-building themes, and this is most evident in the consistent quota policies in commercial television and radio, and amongst the public broadcasters. By the 1990s, dual strategies that spoke of both cultural protection and economic value (McLeay 2006) were evident even as deregulation policies were rolled out across the media industries. This was possible whilst older certainties held, primarily continuity about where audiences could be found, and stable times and spaces (and revenues) of consumption and production.

These former certainties are now on shakier ground. Policy enquiries are now reflecting the popular music industries' disquiet about the disproportionate share of federal government funding allocated to the traditional arts. It is expected that when the embattled Labor government finally announces its response to both the National

Cultural Policy submissions and Australia Council review, that 'contemporary music' will be more prominent in revised funding strategies. This would be in keeping with the views expressed by many within both classical and popular industries. In a report, I produced for the Australia Council on the needs of the local recording sector, interviews with classical, hip hop, pop, rock and avant-garde label owners and managers reinforced the operational similarities, rather than discursive divides:

> This is not to say that different art worlds do not exist according to label, artist and genre. Rather, in the context of this study, expertise and knowledge can be shared to provide new forms of thinking. In commercial terms entrepreneurial risk is equally evident in a small hip hop label signing a nineteen year old for her first recording, and in a small classical label publishing a string quartet's original compositions for a small domestic market. In artistic terms, notions of conformity (a classical artist's continuing resort to eighteenth century repertoire, for example) and innovation (pop 'mashups' for instance, that challenge genre histories and techniques) exist across all forms, dependent upon aesthetic traditions that have evolved over many years. (Australia Council 2012, p. 10)

This has been accelerated by the other means by which popular music has become 'useful'. Federal, state and local government funding has been proactive in supporting a range of 'unpopular' (Redhead 1995) music activity. Putting aside claims in some quarters that these genres might be 'un-musical', 'un-Australian' or 'illegal', there has been an acknowledgement that as 'unpopular' music practices, they nonetheless constitute 'a whole way of life' for a sector of music consumers/producers. Hip hop in particular has increasingly been employed at local government levels in a variety of arts, health and youth programmes, and not always without controversy (see Huq 2007).

Conclusion

Despite the recent ring fencing of support for the major arts companies though a federal-state Accord and Major Performing Arts Framework (Meeting of Cultural Ministers Communique 2012), the historical discourse of 'excellence' as the primary focus of support is becoming harder to sustain. As a recent Australia Council report pointed out, this does not have to be an either/or question:

> On the one hand, should the arts be approached purely in terms of state subsidy or are there other policy approaches better attuned to the commercial practices of the creative industries that could be beneficial to the arts? On the other hand, should the creative industries be approached in purely economic terms; if they are central to contemporary culture, how should they be supported to enhance this cultural contribution? (O'Connor, Cunningham and Jaaniste 2011, p. 5)

This echoes arguments elsewhere in 'a shift way from a simple focus on subsidy' (Pratt 2005, p. 18) that is perhaps the greatest legacy of the emergence of the creative industries. It also involves governments being genuinely inter-departmental in the ways they see culture cutting across different spheres of activity, with accompanying shifts in institutional training and innovation that cut across 'pure' and 'applied' cultural forms (ibid., p. 18–19).

The *Convergence Review* reveals these tensions between creative/economic, cultural/national. Its responses in many spheres articulate a sophisticated hedging of positions: retaining traditional broadcasting quotas, whilst removing obligations for new digital forms; proposing a new national regulator of media and culture, which would oversee a range of *self-regulated* industries and agreements; and an emphasis upon an increasingly international cultural landscape that does not define the larger multinationals as 'content service enterprises' obliged to observe due diligence in the distribution and production of local content.

The *Review* makes clear that if we are not already in a 'post-broadcast' world, then we're certainly in a mixed landscape of consumption/production platforms. In the current 'convergent media policy moment' (Flew 2012), government intervention is increasingly in the name of diversity (of carriageways, producers, platforms, ownership). As an industrial narrative, it continues earlier trends; 'in place of the centralized civil service authorities, semi-autonomous agencies and brokers now provide cultural services to client groups within cultural and media industries, generating new consumer relations' (Meredyth and Minson 2000, p. 1376). The sustained court battles between copyright collection societies and broadcasters reinforced the 'diversity' rhetoric, where reliance upon traditional sources of exposure and income mean commercial stagnation or death.

Certainly, the pre-eminent cultural nationalist narrative described earlier in this article fits with a broader, older nationalism that depended 'upon a singular version of history' that was 'incapable of incorporating a multiplicity of identities and histories' (Turner 1994, p. 10). In the absence of a recognisably defined 'Australian sound' that has enabled consistently strong domestic and export sectors, cultural protectionism understandably emerged as the default policy, linked to normative assumptions of the visibility of Australians on screen, stage and on the airwaves. This was reinforced by (weakening) public interest goals of a plurality of activities and voices. Former explicit links of the national as cultural project, and cultural projects as national, have made way for – and are driven by – the wide array of technological, industrial-organisational shifts and the 'definitional wars' that have changed former understandings of 'culture'.

Finally, the historical traces presented here are not intended to fit within a particular academic genre as prescribed by others. It is not, hopefully or simply, a 'lapsarian account' that 'contrasts a prior era in which a pluralistic and civic-minded approach to public policy prevailed to the current epoch, which is presented as one of ascendant and rampant neoliberalism' (Flew 2012, p. 8). Such an era has never existed in terms of Australian popular music. Rather, in re-assessing the changing mixture of aesthetic, political and economic considerations, where and how governments and industries reassert 'the national' remains an interesting question.

Notes

1. In Australia, the Labor Party adopts the US spelling rather than the Labour Party of British reference.
2. Australia has a tripartite system of government, with a federal (national) government co-existing with six state/territory governments (Western Australia, South Australia, Northern Territory, Queensland, New South Wales, Victoria and Tasmania). This is further supplemented by a series of local councils of varying sizes. Whilst the cultural policy structures at state and local levels are important, in this article I will focus primarily on federal structures.
3. 'Conservative' in Australian political contexts in the main refers to the Liberal Party, and the rural party, the National Party (which existed as the Country Party until its name

change in 1975). Both parties have governed in a coalition arrangement in every Liberal Party election win since the 1950s.

4. A recommendation of the McLeay report, the blank tape levy was the proposed funding stream for local music infrastructure. Its failure to materialise was due in part to the federal government's inability to contest tape manufacturers' objections. The High Court of Australia declared the levy to be unconstitutional in 1993.

5. The use of the term 'contemporary music' began appearing in reports in the 1990s in Australia to distinguish from classical and art music forms. In the early 2000s, a Contemporary Music Working Group was formed to represent different industry sectors (see Cloonan 2008).

6. Despite its public disavowal, some *Creative Nation* policies remained part of Howard government policy from its 1998 'contemporary music development' package, principally the continued funding of the Contemporary Music Touring program.

7. Published before the recent Federal Court judgment, it is interesting that the Review believed that 'the principle of regulatory parity suggests that radio-like services on the internet and terrestrial radio services should be treated in a similar manner' (Commonwealth of Australia 2012, p. 78).

References

Allen Consulting Group, 2005. *Let's get this show on the road.* Sydney: Allen Consulting Group.

Ausmusic, 20 May 1994. *Stayin' alive: creating jobs and culture.* Prepared by Sue Gillard.

AustraliaCouncil, 1983. *The Artist in Australia Today. The Report of the Committee for the Individual Artists Inquiry.* North Sydney: Australia Council.

AustraliaCouncil, 1987. *The Australian music industry: an economic evaluation.* Sydney: Australia Council.

Australia Council, 2012. The music recording sector in Australia: strategic initiatives [online]. Available from: http://www.australiacouncil.gov.au/__data/assets/pdf_file/0007/146761/The-Music-Recording-Sector-Report-2012.pdf [Accessed 2 March 2013].

Australian Copyright Council, 28 March 2012. High Court Upholds 1% Cap on Broadcast Royalties for Sound Recordings [online]. Available from: http://www.copyright.org.au/news-and-policy/details/id/2056/ [Accessed 2 March 2013].

Breen, M., 1999. *Rock dogs: politics and the Australian music industry.* Sydney: Pluto Press.

Brophy, P., 1987. Avant-garde rock: history in the making. *In*: M. Breen, ed. *Missing in action.* Kensington: Verbal Graphics.

Catania, P., 21 February 2012. PPCA v Commercial Radio Australia: Simulcasting [online]. Available from: http://www.corrs.com.au/publications/ip-watch/ppca-v-commercial-radio-australia-simulcasting-via-the-internet/ [Accessed 2 March 2013].

City of Sydney, 2008. *Sustainable Sydney 2030: the vision.* Sydney: City of Council.

Cloonan, M., 2008. What's going on? Perceptions of popular music lobbyists in Australia. *Perfect beat*, 8 (4) 3–14.

Commonwealth of Australia, October 1994. *Creative nation: commonwealth cultural policy.* Canberra: Department of Communications and the Arts.

Commonwealth of Australia, 2003. *From industry assistance to productivity: 30 years of 'the commission'* [online]. Canberra: Department of Communications, IT and the Arts. Available from: http://www.pc.gov.au/__data/assets/pdf_file/0019/7237/thirtyyearhistory.pdf [Accessed 12 February 2013].

Commonwealth of Australia, 2010. *Strategic contemporary music industry plan.* Canberra: Department of the Environment, Water, Heritage and the Arts.

Commonwealth of Australia, 2012. *Convergence review final report* [online]. Canberra: Department of Broadband, Communications and the Digital Economy. Available from: http://www.dbcde.gov.au/__data/assets/pdf_file/0007/147733/Convergence_Review_Final_Report.pdf [Accessed 16 January 2013].

Costello, S., 2003. Community music. *In*: A. Scott-Maxwell and J. Whiteoak, eds. *Currency companion to music and dance in Australia.* Sydney: Currency Press, 158–159.

Craik, J., July 2007. *Re-visioning arts and cultural policy: current impasses and future directions*. Canberra: ANU e-press.

Eltham, B., Spring 2010. Culture is bigger than the arts: the need for a progressive arts policy [online]. *Overland*, 200. Available from: http://overland.org.au/previous-issues/issue-200/feature-ben-eltham/ [Accessed 15 November 2012].

Eltham, B., 5 April 2012. Millions for a tiny record label with powerful players [online]. *Crikey*. Available from: http://www.crikey.com.au/2012/04/05/my-cup-of-tea-millions-for-a-tiny-record-label-with-powerful-players/ [Accessed 5 November 2012].

Federal Court of Australia, 2013. Phonographic Performance Company of Australia Limited v Commercial Radio Australia Limited [2013] FCAFC 11 [online]. Available from: http://www.judgments.fedcourt.gov.au/judgments/Judgments/fca/full/2013/2013fcafc0011 [Accessed 2 March 2013].

Flew, T., September 2012. The convergent media policy moment. *Occasional Paper Series, Institute for Culture and Society, University of Western Sydney*, 3 (3), 1–18.

Florida, R., 2002. *The rise of the creative class*. New York, NY: Basic Books.

Frith, S., 1996. *Performing rites: on the value of music*. Oxford: Oxford University Press.

Florida, R., 2007. *The flight of the creative class*. New York, NY: Harper Collins.

Gibson, L., 2001. *The uses of art: constructing Australian identities*. Brisbane: University of Queensland Press.

Gibson, C. and Klocker, N., 2005. 'The 'cultural turn' in Australian regional economic development discourse: neoliberalising creativity? *Geographical research*, 43 (1), 93–102.

Gillard, S., 1990. *Music and young people. Submission to the youth and arts policy development project*. Sydney: Australia Council.

Goldsmith, B., 1 May 2012. Convergence review: missed opportunity with Australian content [online]. *The Conversation*. Available from: http://theconversation.edu.au/convergence-review-missed-opportunity-with-australian-content-6752 [Accessed 2 March 2013].

Guldberg, H., 2000. *The Arts Economy 1968–98: three decades of growth in Australia*. Sydney: Australia Council.

Hall, B., 26 May 2012. Google's tiny tax bill alarms Turnbull [online]. *Sydney Morning Herald*. Available from: http://www.smh.com.au/opinion/political-news/googles-tiny-tax-bill-in-australia-alarms-turnbull-20120525-1za51.html [Accessed 2 March 2013].

Harris, P., 2003. *The Last Party: Britpop, Blair and the demise of English Rock*. Hammersmith: Fourth Estate.

Hesmondhalgh, D. and Baker, S., 2011. *Creative labour: media work in three cultural industries*. London: Routledge.

Homan, S., 91 May 1999. Australian music and the parallel importation debate. *In*: H. Molnar and H. Wilson, eds. *Media International Australia*. Brisbane: Griffith University, 97–111.

Homan, S., 2008. Playing to the thinkers or the drinkers? The sites and sounds of Oz Rock. *In*: S. Homan and T. Mitchell, eds. *Sounds of then, sounds of now: popular music in Australia*. Hobart: ACYS Publications, 19–36.

Huq, R., 2007. Resistance or incorporation? Youth policy making and hip hop culture. *In*: P. Hodkinson and W. Deicke, eds. *Youth cultures: scenes, subcultures and tribes*. Abingdon: Routledge, 79–92.

Johnson, B., Summer 1995. Jazz and the cultural politics of Australian music. Context. *Journal of music research*, 10, 11–26.

Johnstone, D., 2001. *The Wild One: the life and times of Johnny O'Keefe*. Sydney: Allen and Unwin.

Marks, F., 1969. Australia and New Zealand. *In*: P. Ackerman and L. Zhito, eds. *The Complete Report of the First International Music Industry Conference*. New York, NY: Billboard, 230–235.

McGuigan, J., 2005. Neo-liberalism, culture and policy. *International journal of cultural policy*, 11 (3), 229–241.

McLeay, C., 2006. Government regulation in the Australian popular music industry: the rhetoric of cultural protection, the reality of economic production. *GeoJournal*, 65, 91–102.

McRobbie, A., 2002. Clubs to companies: notes on the decline of political culture in speeded up creative worlds. *Cultural studies*, 16 (4), 516–531.

Meredyth, D. and Minson, J., 2000. Introduction: resourcing citizenries. *Behavioural scientist*, 43, 1374–1394.

O'Connor, J., Cunningham, S., and Jaaniste, L., 2011. *Arts and creative industries. An historical overview and an Australian conversation*. Sydney: Australia Council.

Peatling, S., and O'Rourke, J.,29 April 2012. Parliament probes technology price gouge [online]. *Sydney Morning Herald*. Available from: http://www.smh.com.au/technology/technology-news/parliament-probes-technology-price-gouge-20120428-1xrl2.html [Accessed 2 March 2013].

PPCA, 5 June 2011. Radio cap. Phonographic Performance Company of Australia [online]. Available from: http://www.ppca.com.au/ppca-about-us/radiocap/ [Accessed 2 March 2013].

PPCA, 13 February 2013. Artists and labels win court case on radio simulcasting [online]. Phonographic Performance Company of Australia. Available from: http://www.ppca.com.au/IgnitionSuite/uploads/docs/Media%20Release%20-%20PPCA%20Simulcast%20Case.pdf [Accessed 2 March 2013].

Pratt, A., 2005. Cultural industries and public policy. *International journal of cultural policy*, 11 (1), 31–44.

Radbourne, J., 1997. Creative nation – A policy for leaders or followers? An evaluation of Australia's 1994 cultural policy statement. *Journal of arts management, law and society*, 26 (4), 271–284.

Redhead, S., 1995. *Unpopular cultures: the birth of law and popular culture*. Manchester, NH: Manchester University Press.

Rex, D., 1992. Kylie, the making of a star. *In*: P. Hayward, ed. *From pop, to punk, to postmodernism: Australian popular music and culture from the 1960s to the 1990s*. North Sydney: Allen and Unwin, 149–159.

Rowe, D., 2001. Globalisation, regionalisation and Australianisation in music: lessons from the parallel importing debate. *In*: T. Bennett and D. Carter, eds. *Culture in Australia: policies, publics and programs*. Cambridge: Cambridge University Press.

Rowse, T., 1985. *Arguing the arts: the funding of the arts in Australia*. Ringwood: Penguin.

Sexton, E., 13 October 2010. Sound and fury over Copyright Act cap [online]. *The Examiner*. Available from: http://www.examiner.com.au/news/national/national/general/sound-and-fury-over-copyright-act-cap/1967126.aspx?storypage=1 [Accessed 2 November 2012].

Shuker, R., 2003. We are the world: state music policy, cultural imperialism, and globalization. *In*: J. Lewis and Toby Miller, eds. *Critical cultural policy studies. A reader*. Oxford: Blackwell, 253–264.

Smith, C., 1998. Secretary of State's Foreword. *In*: *Creative industries mapping document*. London: Department of Culture, Media and Sport.

Street, J., 2012. *Music and politics*. Cambridge: Polity Press.

Trainor, G., and James, A., May 2012. *Review of the Australia Council* [online]. Department of Regional Australia, Local Government, Arts and Sport. Available from: http://culture.arts.gov.au/sites/default/files/australia-council-review/australia-council-review-report.pdf [Accessed 2 March 2013].

Turner, G., 1994. *Making it national: nationalism and Australian popular culture*. Sydney: Allen and Unwin.

Turner, G., 2001. Reshaping Australian institutions: popular culture, the market and the public sphere. *In*: T. Bennett and D. Carter, eds. *Culture in Australia: policies, publics and programs*. Cambridge: Cambridge University Press.

Wardle, J., 2011. John Wardle. National cultural policy submission [online]. Available from: http://culture.arts.gov.au/submissions/john-wardle [Accessed 2 March 2013].

Watson, D., 2002. *Recollections of a bleeding heart*. Sydney: Random House.

Westbury, M., 15 September 2010. Where the council funding goes – 09/10 version [online]. Available from: http://www.marcuswestbury.net/2010/09/15/where-australia-council-funding-goes-0910-version/ [Accessed 2 March 2013].

Index

Page numbers in *italics* refers to an illustration

Ackerman, B. 13
African-American music/performers 24, 38–9, 40
American Civil War 31–3
American Federation of Women's Clubs 38
amplified music 85
Anderson, B. 17
anthems, national 17
Arts and Humanities Research Council 9
'Aural Renaissance' 81
Ausmusic 112, 113, 114
Austin (Texas) 93, 97
Australia 5, 108–24; artists' incomes 65;
content quotas for broadcasting 115–17;
Convergence Review report (2012) 117–18,
120–1; and copyright 114–15; *Creative
Nation* report (1994) 113; 'excellence'
discourse 110, 111, 113, 118, 119, 120;
funding challenges 118–19; and Industries
Assistance Commission (IAC) 110–11; *Let's
Get The Show on the Road* report (2005)
115; LFN and wind turbines 86–8; linkage
of arts with high culture 109–10; local
recording sector 120; music policy 2, 89,
109–14; music quotas 117, 118; *Patronage,
Power and the Muse* report (1986) 111;
policy construction sites 109–10; PSA
findings into the prices of CDs 113–14; radio
broadcasting 116–17; and rock music 112;
role of broadcasting 116–18; shift from arts
to cultural/creative industries 114–15
Australia Council for the Arts 65, 108, 109,
110, 118, 119, 120; *The Artist in Australia
Today* 111
Australian Federal Police: Sydney headquarters
80, *82*
Australian Film Development Corporation 109
Australian Music Industry report (1987) 111
Australian Performing Group (APG) 62

Barnum, Phineas T. 26
Barry, Brian: *Culture and Equality* 13, 14
Battersby, Dr Jean 63

BBC 14; 6Music channel 10–11; salary paid to
Moyles 11–12
Bennett, Tony 2
Big Society agenda 16
Bikindi, Thomas 18
Blair, Tony 114
Bordwell, Warren 36–7
Bostridge, I. 12
Bourdieu, Pierre 65
Bowery concert saloon (New York City) 32
Britain 9; Blair's arts policy 114; cultural/
creative industry policy 114; cuts in arts
funding 50; licensing laws and live music
19; live music scene 98; local music industry
policy 93; music policy 2; *see also* BBC
British National Party 18
Broadway 31, 32
Burstall, Betty 62

C-weighting: and LFN 85
Calgary Arts Development (CADA) 99–100
Calgary (Canada) 4–5, 92–3, 94, 98–102, 105;
barriers and challenges to developing local
music industry 98, 100, 101, 105; Juno
Awards (2008) 99; local music industry
policy 92; loss of Warehouse 101; music-
related initiatives 100; National Music Centre
initiative 100; and New Black Centre 101
Can Can *33*, 35, 36
Canada: arts funding 118; federal cultural policy
94; involvement of municipal governments
in film and television production 96–7;
municipalisation of cultural policy 96
Canada Music Fund 93
Canadian music industry 92–107; Calgary *see*
Calgary; copyright policy 95; identification
of sound recording with 94–5; lack of
municipal involvement and reasons 93,
95, 98; live music 95; music policy 93–4;
and nationalism 94; reasons for municipal
governments supporting local music 96;
Toronto *see* Toronto

INDEX

Canadian Radio-Television and Telecommunications Commission (CRTC) 94–5
Chevigny, P. 17
Chong, Rose 61–2
Chumbawamba (band) 19
Cincinnati: anti-variety campaign 35–6
Circus Oz 62–3, 75, *76*
cities: creative 64–6, 77; popular music in 4
Clinetop Sisters *34*
Cloonan, Martin 3, 44
Cocker, Jarvis 10–11
Cohen, M. 13
Cole, Nat King 38–9
Colonna Troupe *29, 30*
Commercial Radio Australia 116–17
Comparative Constitutions project 17
concert saloons (United States) 32–3
Conservative Party 16
constitutions: and music 17
contingent valuation (CV) approach 12–13, 15
Convergence Review report (2012) (Australia) 117–18, 120–1
Coombs, H.C. 'Nugget' 109, 110
copyright law 15, 18–19; Australia 114–15; Canada 95
cost benefit analysis (CBA) 10, 12
courts: and music 18
Craik, J. 112
Crean, Simon 109, 118, 119
creative city 64–6, 77
creative class 65, 66, 75, 96
Creative Industries Agreement Implementation Group (CIFAIG) (Scotland) 46
creative industry policy 2, 114–15
Creative Scotland 3, 44–5, 48, 49, 52, 53, 56; *Investing in Scotland's Creative Future* 45; tender for Music Sector Review 46–7
criminal courts 18
cultural city planning 2
cultural policy: definition 2; political nature of 3, 7
cultural rights: and music 21
culture: funding of 13–14; politics and the value of 9–10

De Botton, A. 61
democracy 8, 13, 14
Denmark: and LFN 86
Department of Culture, Media and Sport (DCMS) 9
diversity, musical 14–15
Dixon, Andrew 45
Dworkin, R. 13, 14

Economic and Social Research Council (ESRC) 9
Ekos 48, 49

Environmental Protection Agency (EPA) 83
Esplanade Hotel (St Kilda) 63
Etherington, Dr John 87–8
European Music Office (EMO) 16

Farage, Nigel 19
Florida, Richard 65, 75, 96, 114–15
Frey, B. 12–13
Frith, Simon 47, 48, 55, 56; *Performing Rites* 15

Gaines, Jane 15, 18
Garrett, Peter 118
gentrification 63, 65; and Melbourne indie scene 75, 76, 77
Green Book 10

Hackworth, J. 75
Harvey, David 64
Hawke, Bob 112
Hawkes, Jon 62
Hebdige, Dick 60
Hesmondhalgh, D. 2
Hewson, John 113
Homan, Shane 5, 108
Howard Coalition government (Australia) 114
HUAC hearings 39

indie (independent) creative subcultures 4, 59–78; contribution of 59; and creative cities 64–6; definition and characteristics 60–1; marginality of 64; Melbourne scene 4, 61–3, 66–77; threats to 63–4
Industries Assistance Commission (IAC) (Australia) 110–11
intellectual property law 18–19
International Criminal Tribunal for Rwanda 18
International Music Industry Conference (1969) 108
iPods 81

jazz 39; opposition to in 1920s America 38
Johnson, Bruce 4, 79

Keat, R. 14
Keating, Paul 112, 113
Kelly, Paul 63
Kruse, Holly 54

La Mama Theatre (Melbourne) 62, 63
Lange, David 111–12
law: intellectual property 18–19; music and making of 19; and nineteenth-century American theatre 25–31
Ley, D. 60, 65
LFN (low-frequency noise) 4, 83–6; and amplified music 85; and C-weighting 85; and Denmark 86; factoring of in music regulation policies 86; social impact of 84–5;

INDEX

trauma associated with 84; and Ubiquity Effect 83–4

liberal political theory 13

licensing/licensing laws 3, 19; nineteenth century America 25, 26

live music: Canada 95; Scotland 51, 52, 53; Toronto 103, 104, 105; and UK licensing laws 19

local music policy: Britain 93; Canada *see* Canadian music industry; United States 93

local radio station 4

low frequency noise *see* LFN

McAlpine, Ken 87

McCarthy, Senator Joseph 39

McGuigan, J. 65

Manchester Institute of Popular Culture 54

Manifesto for Music in Scotland, The 16

manifestos, party 16

Marcus, Greil: *Lipstick Traces* 60

markets 20–1

Melba Records 119

Melbourne 93; funding sources for arts-oriented activities 66–7

Melbourne indie scene 4, 61–3, 66–77; and gentrification 75, 76, 77; initiatives and reforms 75–6, 77; location of activities 69–74, *69–73*; profitability and curatorial policy 67–8

Mercer, Colin 2

Miami 93

Michel, Jean-Francois 16

Michigan 36–7

microphone 81

Miles, S. 92

Mill, J.S. 8

Minogue, Kylie 112

Mollett, Richard 55

Montreal 94, 96, 97

Moore, Clover 80

moral reform societies: nineteenth century America 28–31

Moyles, Chris 11–12

municipal interventions: in Canadian music industry 92–107

music: as a commercial product 8; and cultural rights 21; political argument for 13–15; political constitution of 15–21; and urban space 80–6; value of 7–23

Music Calgary 99–100

Music Canada 95, 103, 105

music hall 3 *see also* variety halls

Music Reference Group (Scotland) 46

music volume: regulation of 82

Netherlands: and LFN 85

New Black Centre (Calgary) 101

New Orleans 25, 37

New York City: segregation of amusements 37; and Society for the Reform of Juvenile Delinquents 29–30

New Zealand: arts funding 118

Nijmegen 86

nineteenth century America 3, 24–43; anti-variety campaign in Cincinnati 35–6; attempt to shut down Bordwell's theatre in Saginaw 36–7; Can Can *33*, 35, 36; concert saloons and law against 32–3; continuity of logic of into twentieth-century 37–40; economic depression (1870s) 33–7; economic recessions 30; hostility towards theatrical entertainment 25–6; licensing laws 25, 26; moral reform societies 28–31; segregation of entertainment into designated districts 37; tableaux vivant exhibitions 26–8, *27*; theatre law 25–31; variety halls 31–2, 33, 35–6; vaudeville 34

noise pollution 4, 19, 79–91, 82; and low-frequency noise *see* LFN; and pitch 82–3; and Sound Pressure Level 86

Norman, Jesse 14–15, 16

Norwich 93

Nussbaum, Martha 8

O'Brien, Dave 9–10, 12, 92

Ofcom: and pay-to-play 20

Offenbach: *La Vie Parisienne* 35

O'Keefe, Johnny 110

Ontario Media Development Corporation (OMDC) 102

Ontario music industry 102, 104

opera, funding of debate 13

Opera House (East Saginaw) 36

Paquette, J. 96

Parents Music Resource Center 41

party manifestos 16

pay-to-play: and Ofcom 20

personal stereo systems 81

Phonographic Performance Company of Australia (PPCA) 116

pitch 82–3

pneumothorax 84

Policy Notes: Popular Music, Industry and the State conference (2012) 1–2

political movements/organisations: and music 15–16, 18–19

politics: and the value of culture 9–10

Popular Music Studies: cultural studies turn in 56–7; involvement in shaping of policy by academics issue 54–5

Porter, L. 66

Pram Factory (Melbourne) 61–2, 63

Presley, Elvis 39

Prices Surveillance Authority (PSA): *Inquiry into the Price of Sound Recordings* 113–14

PSB (public service broadcasting) 11, 14

INDEX

radio/radio broadcasting 38; Australia 116–17
rap: reaction to 40
Redesdale, Lord 19
referenda 13
Reid, Dick 39
rock music: and Australia 112
rock and roll: negative reaction to 39–40
Rock, Terry 99
Rodger, Gillian 3, 24
Rose, D. 74
Rowse, Tim 110
Royal Society of Edinburgh 16
Rwanda 18

Saginaw (Michigan) 36–7
Said, Edward 54
Sancton, A. 96, 97
Sandel, M. 8; *What Money Can't Buy* 20–1
Santorum, Rick 37
Schlesinger, Philip 54, 56
Scotland 3–4; and Creative Scotland *see*
  Creative Scotland; independence referendum
  (2014) 50
Scotland music/music industry 44–58; concerns
  52; and education 51; establishment of Music
  Reference Group 46; geographical issues
  51; involvement of Popular Music Studies
  academics in shaping policy issue 54–6; live
  music 51, 52, 53; *Mapping* report (2002) 47–
  8, 53; numbers employed in 51; and Steering
  Group review 48–53, 54; ticketing sector 51
Scottish Artists Union 45
Scottish Arts Council 44
Scottish Creative Industries Partnership
  (SCIP) 45–6
Scottish Enterprise 47
Scottish Music Industry Association (SMIA) 46
Shaw, Kate 4, 59, 66
Sheffield 93
Sinatra, Nancy 18
Sioux City (Iowa) 38
6Music channel 10–11
Smith, N. 65, 75
Snelbaker, Thomas 36
soap opera: PSB provision of 14
Society for the Reform of Juvenile Delinquents
  (New York City) 29–30
Sound Pressure Level 86
South Africa 18
Springsteen, Bruce: price of concert tickets 8,
  20–1
Stahl, Geoff 61
Steering Group (Scotland) 48–53, 54
Straw, Will 97
Street, John 3, 7
sudden arrhythmic death syndrome 82

Supreme Court (US) 17
Sutherland, Richard 4–5, 92
Swedish Pirate Party (SPP) 16
Sydney 80; Vanity Fair Hotel 80–1, *81*

tableaux vivant exhibitions 26–8, *27*
television 38
theatre law: nineteenth century America 25–31
theatre, nineteenth-century American *see*
  nineteenth-century America
Throsby, David 65, 111
Timlin, John 62
Titan Music Group 103, 105
Toronto 5, 102–4, 105; *Accelerating Toronto's
  Music Industry Growth* report 102–4; film
  production 104; live music industry 103,
  104, 105; local music industry policy 92,
  102–3; municipal government involvement
  in film/television production 96–7; position
  within Canadian music industry 104; sound
  recording industry 104, 105; strengths 102
Toronto Film and Television Office 104
Treasury 10
Tusa, John 9

Ubiquity Effect 83–4
UK Independence Party (UKIP) 19
UK Music 20
United States: First Amendment 17; local music
  industry policy 93; *see also* nineteenth-
  century America
urban space: and music 80–6

value of music 7–23
Vancouver 94, 96, 98
Vanity Fair Hotel (Sydney) 80–1, *81*
variety halls: nineteenth century America 31–2,
  33, 35–6
vaudeville: nineteenth century America 34
Vine Street Opera House (Cincinnati) 36

Wadlow, C. 18
Wardle, John 118–19
Warehouse (Calgary) 101
Warner, Joan 116
Watson, Don 113
Weintraub, A.: *Music and Cultural Rights* 21
West, Gary 49
Wilde, Oscar 18
Williamson, John 47, 55, 56
Willis, E. 8
wind turbines: and LFN 86–8

Young, I.M. 60

Zednik, A. 65